The
Freelance
Mum

The Freelance Mum

A flexible career guide for better work–life balance

ANNIE RIDOUT

4th Estate • London

4th Estate
An imprint of HarperCollins*Publishers*
1 London Bridge Street
London SE1 9GF

www.4thEstate.co.uk

First published in Great Britain in 2019 by 4th Estate

1

A catalogue record for this book is available from the British Library

ISBN 978-0-00-831363-0

The information in this book is for general guidance only and is
not legal advice. If you need more details on your rights or legal advice
about what action to take, please see an advisor or solicitor.

Printed and bound by CPI Group (UK) Ltd, Croydon, CR0 4YY

MIX
Paper from
responsible sources
FSC™ C007454

This book is produced from independently certified FSC paper
to ensure responsible forest management.

For more information visit: www.harpercollins.co.uk/green

For Joni, whose birth prompted me
to change the way I work

Contents

The
Freelance
Mum

Introduction

I've been a freelance mum for the past four years and for me, it works very well. I'm the primary caregiver for my children, but I also support myself financially and contribute to the overall household income. I can afford to buy food and clothes for myself and my kids and I can save up for family holidays. The main issue for me when I first went freelance – at least initially – was money; you don't have that lovely set lump sum appear in your bank, miraculously, at the end of each working month like a PAYE employee does. However, as I discovered, there are ways to secure a reliable income and establish some financial stability when you work freelance as a mum, and I'm going to teach you how.

This book will walk you through the necessary steps to setting yourself up as a freelance mum. From deciding on your career path to launching a website, social media, getting your name out there and perfecting your brand. I've also included a comprehensive guide to the childcare options available to freelance working mums, suggested daily routines for optimum productivity, as well as tips on establishing and maintaining healthy work–life boundaries. Using my own experience, alongside tips and advice from a multitude of other mums who have successfully made a freelance career for themselves, I'll show you that with hard work and determination, any mother can thrive as a freelancer.

So, why go freelance?

Freelancers were worth £119 billion to the UK economy in 2016.

There are 4.8 million self-employed workers in the UK, making up 15.1 per cent of the UK workforce – and we've almost all chosen it for the same reason: flexibility. You can decide your own hours and avoid the slog of a daily commute. But the 79 per cent increase in freelancing mums over the past ten years[1] speaks volumes about where women stand in terms of work and family. Many of us are keen to continue developing our careers after having children, but only if we can find work that fits comfortably around family life.

This desire to find flexible work might well be the reason why 54,000 women in the UK are losing their jobs each year while pregnant or on maternity leave.[2] The work culture welcomes back new mothers who will continue working just as they did before they went on maternity leave – same hours, some overtime – but request part-time work, and you're out. This is when setting up as a freelancer becomes less about flexibility and more about necessity. With no job to return to following maternity leave, women might register as sole traders, or launch their own businesses that they can run alongside parenting. And these so-called 'mumpreneurs' contribute an impressive £7 billion to the UK economy each year.

It's not always a smooth transition from PAYE employee to freelance mum, but once you're up and running, it really does offer flexibility in terms of fitting your career around your family. I lost my full-time, well-paid copywriting job when I left to have a baby, which led to something of a career and identity crash. But I soon realised that my

9–6 Monday–Friday job in east London would have been incompatible with the type of mother I wanted to be. So I flipped my panic into productivity, and when my daughter turned one I launched a digital parenting and lifestyle magazine called The Early Hour.

Three years in, The Early Hour reaches 100,000+ parents a month. I've learned how to monetise my online platform and build a career for myself around it – including writing freelance articles for the *Guardian*, *Red Magazine*, *Stylist* and *Metro*. I've appeared on BBC radio and TV, and I spoke at *Stylist* Live alongside celebrity chef Jasmine Hemsley and the founder of Propercorn, Cassandra Stavrou. The Early Hour has acted as a springboard for me; leading to lucrative consultancy work, well-paid copywriting gigs and being made a partner at women's app, Clementine. This has been my way of sticking two fingers up to the company who employed me as a copywriter but thought I'd become useless as soon as I gave birth. It was my way of saying, 'you can take away my job but you can't take away my power'.

That's not to say it's been easy. It hasn't. I've had to learn everything from scratch: accounting, building a website, SEO (getting my website to the top of

Google searches), how to do PR – after working out what PR actually is – networking, making contacts, social media, how to monetise my website . . . Basically, everything that running a small business entails. And all while looking after my two children, who are now aged four and one. But I quickly discovered that motherhood can give women the incredible tool of productivity; you find ways to squeeze work into tiny pockets of time you didn't even know existed before kids came along.

The thought of leaving behind a salaried job, shared office and daily briefs might feel scary, but if you're keen to spend more time at home than at work, this is probably the path for you. You might have clients or colleagues you collaborate with in some way, but ultimately, you are the boss. You decide your dress code, what hours you'll allocate for work and how much time you'll spend with your kids – or doing yoga, or going for a run. There will be no one checking whether you're back from your lunchbreak on time. If you want to spend all day with your kids then work in the evenings once they're asleep, that's totally viable.

Ultimately, there is no easy option when it comes to balancing motherhood and a career. Leaving your child at nursery when you go off to work isn't easy. Parenting full-time certainly isn't easy. But freelancing, as a mum, might just be as close as you can get to finding a comfortable, guilt-free, work–life balance.

1
Getting started as a freelance mum

What should my freelance job be?

You've decided to take the plunge and go freelance. Perhaps you've left behind a salaried job and want to find work to fit around your kids. Maybe your contract ended when you gave birth, as it did for me. Either way, well done for making this decision. It won't be easy but it will be fun, as long as you're working in a field that excites you. So, how to decide on your freelance path?

An exercise I like to do every New Year's Eve is to envisage the coming year. What would I like to achieve? I think about my career, my family, my social life, my hobbies – everything. And I spend an hour drawing and writing up a detailed plan of my dreams. At the end of 2016, this list included having a second baby, writing articles for the *Guardian* and *Stylist* and continuing to spend lots of time with my daughter. All those things happened. As 2017 came to a close, I created a visual representation of my dreams for 2018, which included earning £100,000 and writing a book.

This exercise could help you to decide what you'd like your freelance life to look like. So ask yourself the questions below, then write a list, draw a picture, cut photos out of magazines and create a collage or write a story – whatever feels most natural to you. Committing your intentions to paper makes them much more likely to come to fruition. It's about having a clear focus and knowing what you're working towards.

In a dream world:

How many days a week are you working?

What are you doing?

How much are you earning?

Are you alone, or surrounded by people – a team, perhaps?

Where are you working from: your kitchen, a shared workspace, a snazzy office?

How much holiday will you take?

Where will you go?

What will your weekends look like?

Remember, this exercise is about everything you'd like to happen. A common barrier for mothers in terms of establishing a new career path is confidence. Many of us find ourselves questioning our identity after giving birth. You look and feel different; people might suddenly treat you as if you're less capable in the workplace. But you're not. You have skills and experience, and now you're going to put them to good use. So, envisage the lifestyle you'd like to lead, think about your skillset and start planning your dream freelance career.

Francesca McConchie (@cakeofdreams) was working as a PA before having her first baby but she wasn't happy in her job, wanted to be around more for her children and was fed up with paying extortionate childcare fees. She'd been a passionate baker for years, and had always been complimented on the cakes she'd made for her kids' birthday parties, so when she started getting enquiries from people who had attended the parties, she decided to start making cakes alongside working as a PA. Once she'd realised how little she was making from her desk job after childcare costs, she decided it wasn't such a terrifying leap to give cakes a go full-time, so she quit the day job and launched Cake of Dreams – her one-woman baking business. She works while her kids are at school – admin and emails on Mondays, then baking the sponges and making different aspects of the cakes towards the end of the week, usually for collection Friday to Sunday. 'I do have to get up early on Saturday (and sometimes Sunday) mornings nine times out of ten to decorate them, which kind of sucks,' she says. 'But it's easier now the kids are a bit older and hanging off my legs less!'

Lauren Davies (@thisisheka) trained as a designer at the prestigious Royal College of Art and worked part-time in studios before becoming pregnant with her son, Max. When he was three months old, she had her work exhibited but realised that the pressure of producing original designs while looking after a young child was too much. Instead, she began using her hard-earned knowledge on sustainable design and started to offer this out as a consultant. She was picked up by a forward-thinking agency and began to work two days a week from home – managing with a mixture of paid-for childcare and utilising Max's nap times. With a high day-rate, this two-day working week enables her to lead a financially comfortable life, while being very much involved in her son's early years.

Anna Jones – bestselling author, cook and columnist for the *Guardian* and *The Pool* – wanted a freelance career that would fit well around motherhood, but also offer variety. 'I've spent my whole life trying to avoid routine,' she says, 'which has been a challenge since entering motherhood, as babies like routine. But I can get bored quite easily. I don't like doing the same thing again and again, so I designed my career so that every day is different. I thrive on that. I'm quite good at being present, which is a good trait for someone who freelances – I'm not worried about where the money's coming from or what I'm doing each month, I'm just living in the moment.'

For Dr Pragya Agarwal – designer, entrepreneur, journalist and TEDx speaker – it was a different set of circumstances that led to her embarking on her multi-skilled freelance career. 'Becoming self-employed was not a decision that I took lightly,' she says. 'After a career at the top of academia, and facing workplace bullying, stress and burnout, I took a difficult decision to take a break and step away from something that I had worked very hard to achieve. I defined myself through that success and that position, and so this change brought about some loss of self-esteem, confidence and a sense of direction. But it also gave me an opportunity to evaluate what I really was passionate about and wanted from my life, and that was to make a positive change and impact and create a life filled with meaning and purpose that was flexible and gave me back control.' She now has multiple income streams. 'This kind of portfolio career suits me because it makes life really interesting and exciting. It has also been good for my mental well-being, as it helps me to keep thinking outside the box and more creatively.'

Whether you turn a hobby into a career, like Francesca; use your experience and knowledge of your industry to offer consultancy, as Lauren does; set up your own shop or small business, like I have; transition into a new but connected phase of your career, like Anna – from chef to food stylist and writer; or find yourself needing a fresh start following an unbearable work situation, like Pragya; it's about ensuring that you are honing in on everything you've learned up until now. You have valuable assets, whatever your previous line of work. So once you've worked out what they are, and what your work–life balance should be, you can start making this your reality. All the practical stuff, like childcare, can be considered later. This initial exercise is just about you and your dream freelance career.

Helen Thorn, one half of the Scummy Mummies comedy duo, says:

'My number-one top tip is to be passionate and love what you do. Don't just choose the style of working because you think you should or because your friends are doing it. Working freelance is wonderful for its flexibility, but you also face other challenges in terms of irregular income, hustling for work and rejection that you wouldn't get in other "normal" employment. If you REALLY love what you do, this will get you through those times.

'One of the most useful things we did a few years into the Scummy Mummies was write down a list of absolutely everything we wanted to do. And I mean everything. And then we chose five to focus on. In the beginning, you'll be tempted to say yes to everything and be "busy". But while the money may be appealing, there are no prizes for exhaustion. Think about your business and brand in the long term and what you really want from it. Being successful is about what you say "no" to, as well as what you say "yes" to.'

Passion work vs money work

Now we can get a bit more practical, because while you may have dreams to be a film actor or novelist, it could take time for this to pay. So in the meantime, it might be helpful to look at your freelance career like a tree. The trunk is you; you're rooted and grounded, standing tall. There are various branches, which might represent the different work you're doing, but at the end of each branch is a flower – that's the end goal. It might look and feel as if the branches aren't connecting, but they are: they are all part of you, and your capabilities, and are linked to your dream career.

For instance, I'm a writer. That's what I love doing. In fact, one my biggest dreams was to write books. But I didn't start my freelance career as a published author, that was going to take time. Instead, I sought copywriting work, which paid well. I didn't have to feature it in my portfolio – some work can just be money work – but I did have to see it as being worthwhile. I focused on the fact that it would be good practice for my later book-writing, as I was finding ways to say a lot in very few words. And I soon learned how to do it.

In time, I built my website, The Early Hour, and this involved editing as well as writing, but also all the techy stuff, social media, cold-calling companies and persuading them to advertise with me. It was loads of work that felt like it veered far from the end goal – writing a book – but they were all branches on my tree. What happened was that I grew a community, and a platform, and this led to me eventually having a pitch accepted by 4th Estate publishers, and the offer of a book deal.

On my journey, I've occasionally been asked to do work that I don't enjoy – like writing the copy for a company whose ethics are questionable, or doing PR for a product I don't believe in. If I've been incredibly strapped for cash, I've taken on the work, but now I'm a lot more selective. Experience gives you the freedom to turn down work, which is a wonderful position to be in. The goal is to spend the bulk of your time doing exactly what you love doing: writing, speaking, acting, making music, illustrating, designing, lecturing – whatever it is, you will be able to do almost solely that. Keep those roots watered and the branches strong and, in time, the flowers will bloom and thrive.

Anya Hayes (@mothers.wellness.toolkit) was a managing editor in book publishing before being made redundant. She went freelance temporarily as an editor, because she didn't have a job to move on to, but also trained as a Pilates teacher at the same time. She was then offered a temporary, self-employed, two-days-a-week desk editor role at Macmillan publishing on a wellbeing imprint. So she did this, while continuing with her training, then stayed in the role while also starting up as a Pilates teacher. It worked really well in terms of balance, though 'not too well in terms of career progression,' she says. The job with Macmillan ended, she found work with another publisher and then became pregnant, which, being self-employed, was financially tricky. Since having children (Anya now has two), she's worked as a freelance editor, Pilates teacher and has written a book: *The Supermum Myth*. A 'cobbled-together' career, says Anya, but one that works in terms of its flexibility, which allows her to work around family life.

Katie Stockdale (@peaceloveandbirth) had been working in fashion before she left to have her baby, but she decided that her maternity leave would be a good time to re-train. So after nine months Katie completed a hypnobirthing course to become a teacher. She then decided she wouldn't be returning to her previous fashion job at all, so she also trained as a yoga teacher. Of the two, hypnobirthing is more lucrative, though she is breaking even with the yoga. To supplement her more holistic work, Katie is a part-time college lecturer on a fashion-buying course. This balance of regular work related to her previous career, alongside embarking on an entirely new career path, is a great example of how you can utilise your existing experience while also trying out something new.

Anna Jones (@we_are_food) trained as a chef under Jamie Oliver. She was then employed as part of a small team, experimenting with cooking dishes and food styling. In time, she started writing bits for the website. All of this was before Jamie had a huge empire and employed specific people for each aspect of it, which was great for Anna, as she got to try her hand at various career paths stemming from food. Interestingly, from a young age Anna knew she wanted to be a chef but also knew it wouldn't be compatible with the family life she dreamed about, and this, in terms of her career direction, was a big drive. 'I knew kids were a way off but I couldn't see how those two things would ever resolve and work together. I still don't understand how mums do it – that's why there are so few at the top of kitchens. You can never be home for bedtime.' So from the get-go Anna was writing alongside food styling as and when in the hope that one day she'd be able to work from home as a freelancer: writing cookbooks (she's now had four published), a column (she writes one for the *Guardian* and another for *The Pool*). This combination is now her full-time job, which fits nicely around looking after her two-year-old son.

Mollie McGuigan has two children, aged four and one. She left her job as deputy editor of the free daily email website, Emerald Street, after the birth of her second child and she's now a freelance journalist. 'Earlier this year I stopped saying yes to every bit of work I was offered and started being more strategic in the work I accepted and pitched for,' she says. 'I want a body of work that represents my strengths and interests, a portfolio that has clear direction. It's meant that I am much more focused and immersed in one area, which has been great for developing ideas and networking. However, it's also meant I've had less work, which has been dispiriting at times. I try to make the quiet times productive: pitching, updating my portfolio, chasing invoices, reading news and features endlessly so I feel tapped into the world, and often it sparks ideas.'

• •

Think big but start small

My dad is an optician and ran a small chain of his own shops when I was growing up, but before that he tested people's eyes from the bedroom of his and my mum's flat in the evenings, while working for an established optician in the daytime. He knew that he needed customers if he was going to start his own business. In time, he was able to open his first shop, round the corner from that flat. All the customers whose eyes he'd tested in his bedroom joined him at his new opticians. He did the building work and painting himself, and called in favours from friends. My dad didn't have start-up funds so he had to keep everything as cheap as possible. Once he was making a profit, he was able to re-design the shop then buy a second one. He grew that business, too, and a few years later he bought a third shop.

He told me about an old friend of his who had also decided to start a business. This guy wanted to be his own boss. My dad advised him to be frugal, at least at the start, and perhaps to even stick with his existing job while trialling the new line of work. Get some clients before you commit to an office space. But this guy didn't want to hear it; he invested in a fancy central London office and bought a nice car to impress clients. Only, he never got any clients, so the business failed and that was the end of his dream to work for himself.

When you're finding your feet, keep your spending to a minimum. Whether you're starting out as a freelancer or launching a new business, if you're able to set it up from your kitchen table (or sofa/bed), do. I'm now earning enough to pay for a shared workspace, but for me, it's more important that I keep building my business and freelance career, so I'm still working from a corner of the kitchen table and spending that money in different areas. If I get bored and need a change of scenery, or if my husband's looking after the kids and I don't want them to distract me, I pop to a local coffee shop that has wifi.

You might be tempted to spend money on smart clothes when meeting potential new clients. Of course presentation is important, but don't get carried away; you can look smart without blowing a month's income on a designer jumpsuit. If you keep your hair washed, your shoes clean and your clothes ironed, that's probably enough. It's more important that your personality shines through with your clothes than your income. You're no more likely to get the pitch in an Armani suit than I am in my £35 Lucy & Yak dungarees. In fact, spending a small fortune on clothes when you have young kids is a waste of money; I bought a lovely pastel-pink cashmere jumper for a talk I was doing and it was soon destroyed by my children's mucky hands and tugging. So now I'm back in my high-street clothes and affordable ethical brands.

Put simply: don't spend all your money before you've made it.

Holly Tucker MBE, founder of Holly & Co, co-founder of Not on the High Street, launched the now multi-million-pound business from her kitchen table in 2006. I asked how she managed childcare in the early days. 'He was with me, sleeping under the table!' she says. 'I look back on those days with such fondness, because he grew with me and my business in those early years. It was funny, because with launching Holly & Co came more years of hard days and late nights, and Harry was there again, sleeping under the table. My biggest supporter.'

Ask any entrepreneur or superstar freelancer and you'll hear the same thing: think big but start small.

• •

Getting the ball rolling

Now that you've come up with your freelance career focus, you need to turn yourself into a brand. Will your freelance work be under your name, or will you create a more general name? For instance, my copywriting and consultancy work is under Annie Ridout (annieridout.com) while my digital magazine is called The Early Hour. Down the line, you might want to expand your services and have other people work for you, so this is worth bearing in mind. That said, Arianna Huffington had no issue turning The Huffington Post, clearly named after her, into a multi-million-dollar enterprise, so if the brand's really strong, and the work is respected, that will be what matters most.

Steve Jobs, founder of Apple, said in his autobiography that the idea for his business name stemmed from him being on one of his 'fruitarian diets'. He'd just come back from an apple farm and thought the name 'Apple' sounded 'fun, spirited and not intimidating'. The name for the BlackBerry phone – the first device that could send and receive emails wirelessly, initially via a pager and later a mobile phone – came about following a brainstorming session with Lexicon consultancy, who are devoted to naming products. Having the word 'email' in the title sounded boring so they looked outside of the box, at unrelated things that make people feel good. Someone suggested 'strawberry' but it was rejected for sounding too 'slow'.[1] 'Blackberry' was suggested, as the device was black and this sounded snappy. The name stuck and the company rocketed.

So it's worth having a good think about names and not choosing anything that will make people pigeon-hole you in the wrong way. I wanted The Early Hour to be for both mums and dads, which is why I didn't use the word 'mum' in the title. I decided on the concept of publishing articles early in the morning, at 5 a.m., for parents who were up with their young babies or kids, and the name followed after a brainstorming session with my sister. We listed everything we could think of associated with mornings, early, parenting, babies – and this one stuck. Well, initially we thought of 'early hours' but there were too many existing brands with this name. And in the end, we liked that it was more rhythmic-sounding and that it was as if 'the early hour' was our hour; we owned it. It also felt this name would still work if the brand expanded to include consultancy, which it has, or other branches of work.

• •

Make it your domain

Before committing to a name for your brand, check whether the domain is available for your website – e.g. theearlyhour.com/annieridout.com – and the social media handles. You can check domains by googling 'domain checker' and using one of the sites that pop up. Ideally, you also want your website name to be your handle. Or if your work is under your own name, try to secure social media accounts with your name (e.g. I'm @annieridout on Instagram and Twitter). There's more on social media in Chapter 6, but for now, I'd recommend Instagram and Twitter for starting out. In terms of finding a business name that you'll be able to own the domain for, you will need to think outside the box. If you choose 'The Mummy Blogger' as your brand name, the likelihood is that both the domain and social media accounts will already have been snapped up. So opt for something more original that you can use across platforms.

When you're checking domains, you can put in the brand name you're toying with, followed by .com and you'll be told whether it's available or already exists. Ideally, you want the .com, as it's good for SEO (getting to the top of Google searches, see page 231) and it's what people automatically type into Google. But if you're totally set on a name and can only get .co.uk or .org or .co, it's not the end of the world. As long as you build a strong brand, website and following, these things will supersede your top-level domain (TLD) – the last few letters of your URL.

• •

Website hosting

Now you'll need to decide where to host your website. I chose to buy my domain through Tsohost – they have great tech support, and were recommended for me. But I've also used GoDaddy, and while they're more salesy, they've been helpful whenever I've had an issue. After buying your domain through one of these websites, you can build it from scratch or use a popular platform like WordPress or Squarespace, that allows you to choose a template and slot in all your information without having to know coding. Also, you'll have full control of your content going forward, which might not be the case if you hire someone to build you a custom-designed website.

The Early Hour is built on WordPress. I had a website whizz friend, Mike Parks, design it, using one of the templates WordPress offer, and a graphic designer friend, Matt Bucknall, design the logo. The two of them worked together to create something I'd like: Matthew did the logo design and the general look of the website – the fonts, features, spacing – and Mike made it happen. They had ideas for little features to add in and make it more original, like the sun that rises as you scroll down when you're looking at theearlyhour.com on desktop computers.

When choosing between WordPress or Squarespace, each has its advantages. I chose WordPress because it's been around longer so there are more web developers who know it inside out, and also there are loads of plugins available. Plugins are used to add new features to your website, like social media icons so people can click straight through to your Instagram account, or sharing buttons. Also, pop-up boxes asking people to sign up to your mailing lists. But some people find Squarespace more user-friendly. Creatives often like Wix, as it's simple to import images and move them around. But if you're selling products, Shopify might be the one for you.

Email address

You should have at least one email address included when you buy your hosting package so that you can have a [yourname]@[yourwebsite].com. This is crucial in terms of looking professional and legitimate. Having sallybluesocks@hotmail.com isn't going to cut it. And to be honest, nor is phoebedavis@gmail.com. Get an email address that fits with your website and makes it clear that you are a professional. I'd recommend having [yourname]@ rather than hello@[yourwebsite].com or info@[yourwebsite].com, as this means that when someone's emailing you; a client you've been in touch with before, they can start typing your name and your email address will appear. They won't automatically think to start trying 'hello' or 'info', so this will save them time and mean they don't have to do the annoying job of finding your last email in their inbox and replying to it.

Tech support

If you're looking for help with the tech side of things and don't have a pal who can sort you out, People-PerHour (peopleperhour.com) is a great website – you add in your job (e.g. I need a WordPress website built/customised) and people will pitch to do the job. You choose who you'd like to work with and agree a fee, then you're off. It's particularly useful if you don't want a long-term commitment but need a job done quickly and professionally. I've used it for adding features to my website, like comments boxes under the articles. And get Google Analytics installed, too. That way you can track all traffic to your website and see where people are being referred from. The bulk of your traffic might be coming from Facebook posts, or tweets, and this is helpful to know, so you can see what you're doing right on that specific platform.

• •

The logo matters

You'll need an original logo, as the ones that come with WordPress templates won't be good enough. If, like me, you're not a designer, call in a favour or pay someone: the visual identity of your brand really matters. Freelance graphic designer Emily Brooks says: 'A logo represents your business in any format – and people will recognise it as your stamp. It's like a barcode, and it enables people to track you across all your platforms. The logo should capture the core; the essence of the brand.' So even if your logo is just one letter, the font and colour and shape will eventually become your visual signature. 'A logo should be versatile,' says Emily, 'it can change over time as your brand evolves.'

When briefing Matthew about the logo for The Early Hour, I said it was a parenting magazine so something playful or that nods to children/family would work well. That it should be unisex, positive and represent the early hours of the morning. He came back with a series of designs – some had a moon in the logo, some had a sun. Interestingly, he'd interpreted 'the early hour' as being both the end of the night and the beginning of the day. But I wanted to appeal to parents who are up early, so I opted for the sun. Also, this felt more positive. I love the logo he designed: it's simple, clean and timeless – it really represents my brand.

On the subject of visual identity, try to avoid using obvious stock images across your website. Either take your own photographs, if you know how to take a good picture, or use a website like unplash.com or designspiration.net where you can find better-quality (free) photographs. Just check whether you need the photographer's permission, or to give a credit. Try canva.com (or the related app), which is great for simple picture editing if you don't have Photoshop. It enables you to create one image containing a selection of photos, so I use it when I have two portrait pictures but need a landscape image for The Early Hour – I put the dimensions in and place the two images side by side. You can choose different backgrounds, or add fonts. This can be useful for creating social media posts (like quote boxes) too.

Branding

Whether you're starting a small business selling products, or offering out your own services, you'll need to think about your brand. This includes the visual side of things: the logo, look of your website, brand colour palette (is your website in simple black and white, pastel colours, or brightly coloured?) but also the ethos. What do you want people to associate you and your work with? Are you an eco-warrior practising in sustainable design? If so, this needs to come across in every aspect of your offerings – the copy you use, the design details, your social media accounts. Or perhaps you want to create a gentle, approachable, personal brand that includes lots of behind-the-scenes shots, talking about things that matter to you – such as family or politics? Think about how you want to be viewed and make sure this runs through every element of your business.

Look at other brands that you admire. What is it that you like about their approach? Perhaps they are trustworthy, or respond quickly to feedback and complaints. Maybe their copy is funny and this adds a lighthearted edge to their brand and services. In everything I do, I aim to be punctual, efficient, reliable and good value for money. I like to be approachable in my manner, so this is reflected in the copy I use on social media and across my websites. Other freelance mums are offering high-end bespoke services or luxury products, so, similarly, this will need to come across as soon as you discover them – online, and in person. If you are your brand, it goes as far as the way you dress when you're networking. What impression do you want to give?

Carrie Anne Roberts, founder of Mère Soeur clothing and accessories brand, started one of the first 'mama merch' businesses; selling t-shirts, totes and badges for mothers. She's built a loyal following on Instagram and runs a tight ship, all while being a single mum to her three-year-old son, River. Carrie shares her branding tips:

i. **REALLY think about what your brand means to you** and what you want it to mean to other people. Keeping your goals and your message in mind will help you stay on track when doubt creeps in or you're making difficult decisions.

ii. **Not everyone is going to like what you do** and that can be a terrifying thought when you've put so much work and effort into building a solid brand. Putting your work out into the world can be scary but don't cave under the pressure or dilute your message or product in order to try to please everyone. Keep your vision and stay focused.

iii. Enjoy it! Brand building can be number/ research heavy but it's also meant to be fun. Don't stress about having everything in place and completely perfect from the moment you start. Allow yourself time to learn and finesse your style as you go along and grow with your brand.

Anna Jones agrees with this organic approach, building her one-woman brand in the same way from her initial vision:

'I had a strong idea of how my food should look – the food pics, and the style of cookbook. Especially when writing about vegetarian food, as there was less of it around at the time. And I didn't want my stuff to be all "hemp trousers and brightly-coloured cafes". I wanted something calm, clean and well considered. So that's what I went for. But I've never had a brand person advise me, it's been really organic. I have a group of friends and people I've worked with, including my sister, whose creative opinion I trust. They're engaged in culture, art and design. So I come up with the ideas I think are right for me, that suit me, then I send that out to a limited group of people and get their opinions. That's how the visual side has grown.'

Spreading the word

You've decided what work you'll be focusing on, bought the domain, built a website, set up the social media channels. Now what? You need to launch: both online and in the 'real world'. After all, no one will know what services you have to offer unless you tell them. If you're a perfectionist (I'm not), you might never feel you're ready to show the world your wares. But remember, you're at the beginning of this journey. You will be tweaking and improving all the time. So bite the bullet, set a launch date and stick to it. Here's how to launch as a freelancer . . .

i. Tell your friends

Hopefully, your friends will be engaged enough with you and your life to know that this has been bubbling up for some time. But don't be afraid to slip it into new conversations. It can feel awkward for some people, particularly introverts – of which I'm one, I'm more comfortable asking the questions than giving the answers – but you need to learn to talk about yourself. It doesn't need to be braggy, just saying: I'm so excited, my website's just gone live! is likely to lead to a conversation about it all. And you'll then be in your pal's mind the next time someone asks her for a recommendation in your field.

ii. And your acquaintances

Facebook is a great way to put out feelers. I often have friends announcing their re-branded website, or newly launched business on Facebook. It will usually be followed with: please have a look and let me know what you think, and a request for any copy errors to be brought to their attention. Putting it out on social media like this means no one's being put on the spot. If someone is interested in your area of work, or in you, they will have a look and give feedback. People tend to like being asked for help – and giving it. It takes so little effort on their part but could be very beneficial to you.

iii. Build excitement on social media

You've set up your social media handles but how do you use your channels to announce that you've launched? Before going live, upload a series of posts. Not too many, because people probably won't go back through and read them all, but enough to create a profile that doesn't look empty and boring. And then do a countdown on all of your channels. This can be a visual countdown – on Instagram and Facebook, with photos of the numbers, counting down from ten days to launch – each day, adding a caption about your business or services, or just about you. Or a written countdown on Twitter.

As an example, let's take Emma Grant. She recently set up a brand called Binibamba, selling sheepskin rugs and buggy-liners.

On Instagram, she uploaded loads of images, ahead of the launch, so that when you visited her profile, it looked like an established brand. There were photos of the beautiful, luxurious sheepskin rugs, cute babies trialling the buggy-liners, all snuggled up, and behind the scenes shots. Emma introduced herself, and the details of her products (e.g. that they are handmade in England, and hand-cut from 100 per cent merino sheepskin. Also, that each order comes with a free 100 per cent cotton dustbag). And then she started a 'launching soon' countdown, getting people excited.

Using Twitter, you can put out a tweet a day, in the lead-up, building the momentum by counting down:

> Only five days to go until my website is live . . . if you sign up to my mailing list now, you'll be entered into a competition to win a sheepskin buggy-liner with which I'm launching my new brand.

> Tomorrow the website will be up and my shop will be open. I'd love to hear from anyone who's on the lookout for the softest, most beautiful, baby-friendly sheepskin buggy-liners . . .

It's about getting people to engage with your brand before you launch. Introducing yourself and your business or services before they are available so that people are thinking: I need a piece of this; I want in.

Do a skills exchange

If you're starting out with little or no budget, one great way to get professional help without taking out a loan is to do a skills exchange. I did this with the photographer Penny Wincer and it worked so well. I'd gone to Penny asking if she'd be able to take some headshots for me. She offered to do it for free, but I said I'd like to pay her – if not with money, then with my skills. After listening to me being interviewed on a podcast, talking about blogging and writing for the online platform, Penny said, would you be able to help me with my blog, looking at the direction I'd like to take it in and how to get there? I agreed, and after doing a photoshoot together, we had lunch and I gave Penny ideas for taking her blog forward (SEO, content strategy, pitching for related articles in nationals). You have skills that could be very useful for other people, so bear this in mind if you're looking for help but can't afford to pay the full price.

Switching from mum mode to work mode and back

If you start out by working when your baby or young child is napping, you'll find yourself cramming a lot of work into a very small window of time. Just as you get really stuck into what you're doing, you'll hear their cries on the monitor. It can make your heart sink. Not because you don't want to see your kid, but because working can feel like such a nice escape and to have it abruptly cut short is frustrating.

So it can then be hard to switch your mind from work back to motherhood. You will inevitably find yourself quickly rattling off an email while giving your baby their post-nap bottle, or popping on *Peppa Pig* for an hour so that you can finish a pitch. I think this is fine, though, don't forget, you're doing this to support your family, and you've chosen a freelance career to fit around family life. It's not selfish, and it won't damage them. I remember reading an article about how work and parenting should always be totally separate and then panicking, as mine were very much blended. I now realise this is OK; it's unrealistic to aim for these two parts of your life to be completely distinct – particularly if, like me, some of your work has a family or parenting focus.

Womenswear designer Kelly Eckhardt agrees. She says that mothers need to feel comfortable with their desire to have a fulfilling career, and that sometimes it will involve work and family time overlapping if there is no childcare in place. 'Don't feel guilty for wanting to succeed in your work,' she says. 'I personally believe kids should see their mothers succeed; this shows them that women can be loving but also intelligent and super motivated. A happy mum = a happy family.' It's for this reason that she advocates occasional screen-time, when necessary. 'It's OK to stick your kids in front of a screen for a little while if you need to finish an email or a write-up. We all do this. It's fine.'

Mère Soeur founder Carrie Anne Roberts says: 'The hardest thing about juggling work as a single mum is, surprise surprise, finding the time to actually work. If I'm not working I feel like I should be and if I am working I feel like I'm not being as present as I could be for River. There is a constant pressure to excel as a parent and in my career but the balance is difficult to achieve. The one thing that makes it all easier is the fact that I can work to my own schedule and be around for River a lot more than I would be if I'd gone back to work 9–5. As difficult as the juggle can be, I'm beyond grateful for the time I have with him and the flexibility I have from this kind of work.'

Dr Jessamy Hibberd – clinical psychologist, TEDx speaker and author – says: 'I split my week – three long days working (with some drop-offs/pick-ups with the kids) and then Thursday–Sunday with my family. I do work when they're asleep when needed, but I don't check emails/work when I'm with them. I think I find it easier to do one thing at a time. When I'm with the kids I'm with the kids. When I'm at my clinic, I'm seeing people, and when I have my non-clinic time I focus on a project.'

Sarah Turner – founder of The Unmumsy Mum blog, author of two *Sunday Times* bestselling books and freelance journalist – says that her biggest challenge is living with the constant fear that she's 'on call' for both work and parenting. 'I never feel like I am doing either job particularly well, as I have a terrible habit of checking work emails when I'm with the kids and checking that the kids are all right when I'm supposed to be working. A big part of this problem stems from the fact that I don't have a separate office or workspace at home and so very often can still hear the kids when I'm writing from our bedroom (and they know I'm there, so often potter in and disturb me!).

'At the moment, my husband is taking shared parental leave after the birth of our third baby and so is not working, which means I am free to do more work, but now I have to contend with everyone being at home pretty much all the time. I have been trying to escape to the local library or co-working spaces to allow for better concentration but that presents its own problems, such as when I need to dial in to a Skype meeting or discuss a confidential project I don't really want to shout about across the library café. I sometimes miss the days of going out to work in the morning, shutting the door behind me and then returning in the evening ready to be "Mum" and not "Mum who's here all the time but always working". The reality is that my new work life is so intertwined with my home life that there can never be a clean break or distinction between the two. In actual fact, it's often our "downtime" that provides the richest material for me to write about and I can't seem to stop my mind from thinking, "I should blog this!"'

If you're keen to close the laptop at some point and become 'mum' again, here are some tricks for navigating the switch from mum to work mode and back . . .

— **Make yourself a cup of tea or a glass of ice-cold water.** Focus on it while you drink. This signals the end of working and back to being a mum. Or the reverse.

— **Clementine app has a 'reset' recording,** which is just five minutes long, that helps you to leave old thoughts behind and move into a new part of your day.

— **Allocate the last 10 minutes of working or childcare to transition.** So if you're at your desk, spend 10 minutes preparing to be 'mum' again: get a bottle ready for the baby, go to the loo. If you've been mum, allow yourself 10 minutes to get into work mode once your child has gone for her nap or to nursery, e.g. read the news on your phone. But don't get sucked into social media.

— **When you've finished work, leave your phone at your desk.** This prevents the temptation to check emails 'just once more' while your child drinks her milk or whatever.

— **Do five minutes of stretching.** If you've been sat at a desk, this will pump energy back into your body, and if you've been with your child, it'll help you to focus on your next task: work.

Most of us are guilty of flicking through social apps on our phones while looking after our kids. If you're starting to feel guilty about this, you could always try one of the apps for creating barriers between being online and offline. For instance, Moment, which tracks all your online time and updates you at the end of the day. Most of us spend far too much time on social, but having it quantified might just be scary enough to enforce some habit changes. It certainly has for me. At times like the nursery pick-up, I used to push the buggy with one hand and scroll with the other. Now I'm trying to leave it in my pocket and just walk. And see. And think. (And respond when my son sticks his hand out for yet another breadstick.)

Courtney Adamo, co-founder of Babyccino Kids – an international lifestyle website for modern mums – and a mum of five, has discovered the importance of separating family life and work life. 'While we (women/mums) are good at multi-tasking and can totally cook dinner, answer emails and hold a baby all at the same time,' she says, 'I have learned from experience that I work better and feel happier (both in general and about the work I'm doing) when I focus on one task at a time and give it my full attention. Especially the part about being a mum. If I am distracted with my kids, they can totally feel it and everything spirals from there in a negative way.'

●●●●●●●●●●●●●●●●●●●●●●●●●●●●●●

Where to work from?

I've always been happy spending time alone, so for me it works to set myself up on the end of my dining-room table and type away with a view of the garden. Also, I found this easier to fit around my children's naps. That said, there were a few months when my son wanted to sleep at the exact same time I had to drop my daughter at nursery, so I'd find myself waving goodbye to her then reclining the buggy and doing some vigorous jiggling until he dropped off. I'd park up by a bench – anywhere – and work on my phone: emails, writing, editing. It wasn't ideal – mostly because there was no toilet. Or coffee. But going into a cafe was going to wake him from his sleep, so in order to best utilise this time, a bench it was.

I now work from home or my local coffee shop, which has fast and free wifi, excellent coffee and nice cheese toasties for lunch. I rack up a bill of around £12, which isn't much considering on my work days I might be there from 9.30 a.m. until 3 p.m. Others prefer to use the local library, a shared workspace – some even come with a crèche (there's a list of these at the end of the book) – or you might be able to make use of the crèche at your gym – half an hour on the running machine, followed by an hour and a half of work.

Something I've recently started doing is borrowing a friend's house to work in. She and her boyfriend are out during the day, Monday–Friday, and they have a cat who likes company. It means I don't have to commando-crawl out of the kitchen when my son comes home from the Toy Library with his child-minder – if he sees me, he doesn't want to be parted again – but I also don't have to pay for coffee. This exchange could work well if you have a friend whose dog needs walking. Or perhaps you could spend your last hour cooking dinner for their return? Worth it, for a free workspace.

Lucy Mangan – *Stylist* columnist, *Guardian* writer, author – says that her greatest challenge as a freelancer is feeling she's doing neither work nor motherhood properly. 'I'd prefer to be doing one thing, as well as I can,' she says. So attempting to work from home while her seven-year-old son is there can create tension. 'Multitasking is not my thing,' she says, 'especially when I'm doing creative writing. I need long, uninterrupted stretches of time. And a quiet space. But as your child gets older, they become more demanding. They want to spend time with you. Of course they do. But this means I can't just shut myself in my study, so now I'm working more outside of the home; in the library. I've also joined a private member's club. It's so lovely to be looked after – people bring you food that you haven't had to cook, and coffee. It's tax deductible so I pay £600 a year for my membership.'

Having somewhere to work outside of the home also removes you from a domestic setting, which can be distracting (laundry to be hung out, packages being delivered, etc.). 'As a freelancer, you need to be more selfish than you feel comfortable with,' says Lucy. 'If I'm in the house, I feel all the domestic duties coming at me. But if I leave the house, they can't intrude on my mental space.' Of course, working outside of the home means you have less control over your surroundings – including noise. 'Always carry headphones and white noise to block out irritating sounds,' she advises. 'It's incredibly frustrating when you plan to work on the train for four hours and end up next to someone playing music loudly on their mobile. But white noise will drown them out. Or you can just ask them to be quiet.'

Dealing with isolation

While I'm generally OK with my own company, there were definitely times – particularly in the dead of winter – when my daughter was at nursery, and before my son was born, when the house felt incredibly quiet, and I longed for some human contact. Sometimes, I'd go to the shop just so that I could have a chat with someone. Or phone my sister. When my son was at home with the childminder, I had to vacate, so I'd work in public spaces, meaning I was surrounded by activity. I still go now, if I feel lonely. Although I don't intend to meet up with anyone – I'm there to work – I've actually made friends at my local coffee shop with people who are also freelance, and there to work. So we'll have a quick chat, or give each other some advice, then get our heads back down. Working in this way – surrounded by other people who are also tapping into their laptops – makes me forget how isolated I sometimes felt when I worked from home.

Sali Hughes – author, columnist for *The Pool*, *Guardian* and *Empire*, and event host – says that the social aspect of office work can be felt as a real loss when you go freelance. 'Lots of women really struggle when they go freelance with the fact that they're not in a team any more. They don't have those water-cooler moments. You have to embrace social media, but know when to stop. Be able to manage the loss of the social aspect.' She used to enjoy managing people in the workplace, as well as coming in and talking about what was on the telly. 'But now I've got Twitter and Facebook for that,' she says. 'After my first baby, it was the isolation that made me go mad. I didn't know anyone with a baby, so I was really lonely. But after my second baby, there was Facebook – then Twitter. So I had people to talk to. As a journalist, if you're a freelancer, it's very solitary. Twitter and Facebook *are* the office. They're your colleagues; people you speak to in place of physical co-workers. But then you're reliant on yourself to stop messing about and get on with work. I strongly advise freelancers to block the internet between certain hours, using software. And if you need bustle, go to a coffee shop.'

Pragya Agarwal – designer, entrepreneur, journalist, TEDx speaker and mum of three, including two-year-old twins – agrees that becoming part of an online community, and using social media for real social interaction, can help to combat the isolation. 'Working from home can be lonely,' she says, 'and I have written extensively for Forbes about how to manage loneliness as a freelancer. There are times when I do not speak to any adult for days, and so it is really crucial for me to have a strong community online. But I also try to go to some networking events when possible.' (If the idea of 'networking' makes you feel panicked, there are lots of tips for making it more bearable – and even fun – in Chapter 9.)

· ·

Say yes

At other stages in this book, I'll talk about the importance of learning to say 'no', but when you're starting up, the big word is YES. Yes, I'd like to tell you about my new freelance business. Yes, I'd like to have a coffee with your sister who's an editor of a women's magazine and might be interested in doing a feature on me. Yes, I'd like you to take some flyers and leave them at your work. Yes, I'd like you to wear one of my tote bags to the networking lunch you're attending. Say yes, and watch where it leads . . . And if you think it might be a good opportunity, but you're not sure how, respond as quickly as possible and say: I love the sound of this and it would be great to talk more about it. It's a way of saying 'yes' without saying: let's do it right this second. Sometimes, you'll need time to think about what you want, or can (with child-care limitations) commit to. You can ensure that you don't let opportunities slip away, without making an immediate commitment.

Sali Hughes was working freelance before giving birth to her two sons, so she was already one step ahead in that she was being commissioned for work as soon as she was back at her desk, post-birth. However, she still felt a certain pressure to always say 'yes', in order to keep her position as the go-to for all things beauty. 'The thing about being freelance,' she says, 'is that if you're a successful freelancer, you'll be fine for work. But there's a degree of accepting work because you need to be the person who does it. So

I've always taken on too much; to cement a position. I'm prone to taking on more than other people – than men, than people on desk jobs. But I've never missed a swimming gala or school concert, so you take the rough with the smooth. I work much harder than someone at a desk job but they don't get the benefit of that flexibility.' So say yes to the opportunities, but decide where your line will be drawn in terms of family commitments.

Meeting potential clients

The above steps – announcing your business on social media, telling your friends and family about it, saying 'yes' to as much as possible – all take you towards securing your first clients. You are the best person to sell yourself: you know the ins and outs of your trade, and you are the face of your brand. From now on, you'll be telling as many people as you can about your business, so you'll need to refine your elevator pitch. This is a way of explaining who you are, what you do and what you can do for them – all in the time it takes to get from the ground floor to the fifth floor, when they will be (metaphorically) getting out.

As I mentioned earlier, my work has various branches. Let's take one: I'm editor of The Early Hour. My elevator pitch, to a potential advertiser on my website – let's say an organic kids' food company – would be this:

> I'm Annie Ridout, founder and editor of digital parenting and lifestyle magazine The Early Hour. I put out articles at 5 a.m., for parents who are up early. I've grown a loyal following of parents who love thoughtful, ethical products. Like yours.

She might then say: Oh really. I'd love to hear more about what you'd charge for advertising but I'm rushing to a meeting. Can I take your email address? THIS IS THE IMPORTANT BIT: say, how about I take yours? This way, you won't risk her forgetting about you and never making contact. Once she's out of the elevator, or has hopped off the train – wherever it is that you are – compose an email: was great meeting you, Laura. Would love to talk more about how we could work together. Let me know when's good to chat.

Also, if you know people working in your industry, offer to take them for coffee, or lunch, as you'd love to hear more about what they do and how they do it. Then tell them about what you're doing. Always ask lots of questions, people will be flattered if you've done your research and know about them and their work. Showing an interest will make them warm to you. Shouting about you and your own work won't. And remember to be open-minded – when you meet clients in their office, be friendly to everyone you meet: there could be someone else within the company looking for your services at a later date.

Mailing list

You need to stay in contact with all these people you're meeting online and in person, and telling about your services, so get their email address and ask if it's OK to add them to your mailing list. This is a valuable asset for any company: being able to land directly in people's inboxes, rather than having to hope they'll see your post on social media. Having a box pop up on your website asking people to subscribe is a simple way to get sign-ups. There's more later on about growing your mailing list, and when and how to contact your subscribers. But in the initial stages, just get people signed up whenever you can (with their permission).

• •

When am I going to work?

Once you have grown your freelance career and have paying clients, you'll be able to decide whether you'd like to commit to paying for childcare for your children. This will vary from parent to parent. But when you're starting up, you'll need to be prepared to work in the evenings, once the kids are in bed and when they're napping (kids' sleep routines are covered in Chapter 3). This also extends to weekends, if you can enlist a partner or grandparents who are willing to help out. Remember, you're right at the start of this journey. It's going to be hard work but it will be worth it when the money's streaming in and you have the option to outsource some of the childcare. Chapter 4 will go into more detail about the childcare options available.

Don't burn out

While it's important to commit lots of time and energy to your freelance work, you will need to practise self-care, too. It's very tiring being a mum, it's very tiring working alongside motherhood, it's very tiring setting up as a freelancer. But you might find it beneficial to re-frame what you consider a 'break' to be. For instance, I was invited to go on a mum and baby retreat in Hampshire recently. It was two days and a night of yoga, healthy food, massages and inspiring activities. It sounded heavenly, but my husband couldn't take two days off work, and it landed on the two half-days my son was with the childminder so I'd have had to still pay her even if he came with me. Someone needed to collect my daughter from preschool. I had a book to write. So I said no.

However, writing a book while continuing to run The Early Hour, write freelance articles and produce commercial copy takes up a lot of my energy. And as soon as I finish work, I'm on mum duty. I don't get a break until they're in bed. And then I open my laptop and work. So really, I don't stop until I go to sleep. But what I've found is that stealing tiny pockets of time for myself makes it all bearable. For instance, I hop in a really hot bath five minutes before the kids to soak alone before adding cold water and pulling them in with me. I go for a 10-minute run in the morning. Once I've finished work in the evening, I read a novel for five minutes before lights out. This is my 'me-time'. I'd love to have the massages and weekend spa retreats but it's just not doable so I find time for myself in smaller, more manageable ways.

BBC documentary presenter Cherry Healey is a single mother to her two kids, aged eight and four. She works three or four days a week, depending on where and what she's filming, and they spend the weekend as a family. 'What I really like is a Saturday with no plans,' she says. 'I'll go out on a Friday after work if I've already missed kids' bedtimes, and I'll go for dinner, with my boyfriend, or go dancing. But Saturdays are about going to the park, iPads, lolling about. Doing the laundry. We very rarely go away for the weekend. Lazy weekends at home are important for my mental health. Sometimes I feel I should be doing more with the kids but one thing I've learned is that it's the times I make loads of effort that they end up crying because I didn't get them something from the shop. Keep it simple, and local.'

Courtney Adamo took full advantage of freelance flexibility and relocated her family from London to Byron Bay, in Australia. She says she has recently realised how important it is to focus on herself sometimes. She does this through exercise (surfing, in fact). 'I feel so recharged and better prepared for work and motherhood when I have allowed myself some "me" time,' she says. 'As mothers, we have so many things to think about – our kids, our jobs, our homes, our husbands/partners, etc. Taking good care of ourselves can become the lowest priority. But it's actually so important.'

Holly Tucker agrees. 'I was once given some advice that has stayed with me for ever,' she says. 'If you run your own business, you have three things in your life: your business, your family and yourself. You can only "do" two of these at any given time, and guess who never quite features? My tips would be: **1. Book time in your diary for you** – schedule it as you would a business meeting, and stick to it at all costs; **2. Know your numbers** – keep on top of every receipt and expense, from Post-its to advertising; **3. Don't be afraid to delegate** – in life and business. It's OK to fall back on your network for help.'

Candice Brathwaite – author, presenter and influencer – has a different approach to me-time: 'When it comes to time off, I like to take mine in chunks. Last year my husband sent me to Barbados by myself for a week. I was very nervous at first but it was the most re-energising experience ever. Now I try to re-create that length of a break once a quarter. You have to commit to making time for yourself.'

· ·

Get used to rejection

My husband is a filmmaker alongside his day job as a builder. He's brilliant and has managed to make a feature-length documentary around his Monday–Friday work and being very hands on with our children. He's now making a second film. When he'd completed the first film, he sent it to someone influential in the film world and she wasn't as positive as he'd have liked. Suddenly, her criticism superseded all the rave reviews he'd had from other influential people. He felt deflated. I totally got it – it's crap when you're hoping for praise but don't receive it. But it made me realise that I've become so comfortable with rejection that it no longer upsets me.

In the early days, if I pitched for an article to the *Guardian* and didn't hear back, I'd be really upset. Why didn't they want to publish my brilliant idea? But I soon hardened up. I realised that 99 per cent of pitches won't get you the job. But 1 per cent will – and that's why you've got to keep going with it. Swallow your pride, take any constructive feedback and continue on your journey. Also, just because one editor doesn't like your idea, it doesn't mean another won't. I've had article pitches rejected by one women's magazine and then picked up – and published – by another. Don't be disheartened when people say no, because they will, but it doesn't mean you or your idea aren't good enough, it means it's not right for them, at the moment.

Staying motivated

You're probably going to spend quite a bit of time alone, which may not be easy. And there will inevitably be dips in your productivity levels. But there are tricks for staying focused and on track and keeping your energy levels high. I always find that fresh air and movement help, so I might stand in the garden for a few minutes or even hang the laundry out – removing myself from the computer usually allows the ideas to start flowing again.

Emily Brooks is a designer, coach and psychotherapist. She says: 'If you're feeling distracted, there will be a reason. Perhaps you can see a pile of laundry out the corner of your eye. I decide to mentally set it aside until the kids are in bed. So I ensure my workspace is clear and tidy, but everything else I ignore. Equally, you could decide that you'll do half now, half later. That way it's less daunting when you finish work.'

Other ideas:

— **Take a break for lunch,** or just have a glass of water. Being dehydrated and hungry are sure to distract you.

— **Exercise:** a brisk walk, a jog, a lunchtime swim, 20 minutes of Pilates using a YouTube video, a dance around the kitchen. Get those endorphins going.

— Use a website like Freedom (freedom.to) to **block the apps or websites that you go to when you start drifting** (Facebook, Instagram, ASOS, etc.) for a certain period of time.

— If you feel unbearably tired or lacking in energy, **stop working. Come back to it later,** if possible, or tomorrow. Do something for yourself, not related to work, instead.

Freelance journalist Mollie McGuigan says: 'If I can honestly say I've done everything I can with work for that day, I go and do something that is absolutely nothing to do with work and reminds me of the benefits of being freelance – like going for a run or getting a manicure or watching an episode of some weird crime drama.'

● ●

Be consistent

It is important to establish your own set of rules in any business – in terms of how you communicate with clients and colleagues, and also with what you're presenting to the world. Decide on your ethical stance and stick with it.

Suzy Ashworth, founder of the Calm Birth School hypnotherapy franchise and a life coach, says that consistency is also important in terms of output, explaining that whatever area you decide to specialise in, you need to show up consistently. 'If you're going to write a weekly newsletter,' she says, 'make sure it's there every week. If you offer to put on the monthly social party for your gang of freelance friends, do it. You're the person who likes to turn up early to meetings with clients so that they are never left waiting? Arrive early. Every time. You need to speak to 10 new leads every day? Don't give yourself a get-out clause. If you want to be known as the person who follows up with all of the clients' orders with a thank you card – do it for every client, every order. There is a saying that the people who get ahead are the people who do the ordinary things extraordinarily well.'

Get organised

Within your email inbox, create folders for website stuff, receipts, invoices, specific projects, passwords, positive feedback. The 'zero inbox' thing (having no messages that aren't dealt with, and then tucked away neatly in the appropriate folder) is not only satisfying but it also saves huge amounts of time when you're searching for one of those emails. In terms of storing shared projects, Trello is a great website (and app).

You can create folders for different sections of your work, e.g. blog, social media, pitches, and have other people access and add to this information. Toggl helps you to organise your time with an online timesheet and Slack is another app for teamwork and sharing documents and ideas.

2
Money

*Tweet from Meagan Fisher Couldwell
@owltastic: Real thing that just happened to me:
I quoted a client a rate, and the project manager
responded with 'how about we triple that,
so it better matches what we've paid our
male designers for the same work?'.
1. This client is heroic. 2. Female designers:
ASK FOR MORE MONEY.*

When starting out, it's easy to slip into the 'portfolio work' trap and to agree to work for free. As to whether it's ever beneficial to work for free; that's up to you. Personally, I found writing news articles for local newspapers for the byline, to kickstart my portfolio and to get writing practice, helped my career. But this was before kids came along, so time was on my side. Though even then, I remember being contacted by a women's organisation and asked if I'd blog for them. It will be to empower women, she said. I asked the fee and she said there wasn't one but that it would be good for my profile. Oh, the irony. (I said no. Rudely. And then wrote an article about how ridiculous the situation was.)

Now, I wouldn't write any article without being paid. However, I will do talks, occasionally, without taking a fee if it's on an issue I care deeply about, I like the idea of being on a panel with the other speakers or it will be good PR for The Early Hour (or this book). But on the whole, I need payment. I spend a great deal of time preparing for events, so how can I afford to commit those precious hours if I'm not being financially rewarded? You'll decide where you stand on this. Maybe you'll do a few unpaid gigs then realise it's not worth your while. Either way, remember this:

You are of value.

Your work is of value.

So, exactly how much is your work worth? This is trickier. Ultimately, it's worth what someone's willing to pay for it. But this doesn't help with pitching for a job. So do your research. Ask other people in your industry what they charge. I've had countless women ask what I'm paid for blogging, copywriting and writing articles, and I always tell them the truth. I'm not in the slightest bit offended by them asking, or shady about what I earn. The only way women will ever earn enough (as much as, or more than, men) is if we're all transparent. In terms of journalism, I'm paid what the publication offers: this is usually a flat fee and non-negotiable, but it varies from publication to publication. In some ways, this is simpler: they tell me what they'll pay, and we agree a deadline. Done.

But when it comes to deciding what you'll charge for your services, there are a few things to bear in mind. Firstly, although you're starting out as a freelancer, you'll be bringing some – maybe a lot of – experience. All the hours you've committed to learning your trade, or to training if you're new to it, count. The more experience you have, the more you can charge. In terms of The Early Hour, I've always set the cost of a sponsored post wherever works for me. It's rarely just based on monthly views, it's more about the brand I've built and the trust my readers have. If I'm advertising a product, they assume I'll be using that product and believe in the company. And they'd be right: I'd never promote a company I don't like or that is morally questionable. So sponsored content works very well. It's for this reason that I can charge £1000 for one article.

But a while back, I wasn't charging so much. I was asking companies to simply cover the time it would take for me to work on creating an article that promoted their product. I wasn't taking into account how many readers I have, the community I've built over the past few years, my writing experience. And then, by chance, I discovered that a blogger whose following was 10 per cent of mine was charging more for sponsored posts. I couldn't believe it. I thought: well done you. And then immediately upped what I charge. This is why we need to talk openly, within the industry, about money. We can help each other to get greater financial reward for our hard work.

Deciding your freelance rate

There are two main considerations when deciding on your freelance rate:

1. What would I like to charge?

2. What will clients be willing to pay?

You may have an amount in your head that sounds like a fair day rate, but what do you NEED to charge? By using a freelancer, the client probably won't be shelling out for desk space, a computer, sick pay, maternity leave, travel. You'll be covering all those costs. This means your day rate will be higher than a full-time PAYE employee's annual income divided into days. Start with what you'd like to earn over the course of a month – to cover bills, childcare, your own expenditure, office costs, travel, phone, internet, everything related to you getting your work done – then divide it by the amount of days you'll be working. And remember that you'll be paying tax on your earnings, too. And that you won't be working 365 days a year. (Well, you might, but it's not advised.)

My monthly outgoings and earnings:

I've allocated two days a week to working, plus the hours when the kids are asleep but I'm not. The way my husband and I work out our finances is that he pays the mortgage and bills, and I cover childcare, food, clothes for me and the kids. It works out that we're each covering roughly the same amount each month. He works full-time, Monday–Friday, so this might sound unequal but I've chosen to work less-conventional hours – evenings, nap-times, weekends – so that I can be with my kids midweek. Sometimes I work more than 40 hours a week, but I enjoy it so I don't mind that for now I'm sacrificing evenings and weekends, and working unsociable hours. It's my choice. And it works for our family.

My costs each month:

£400 for my son's nursery fees

£600 a month food for the family

£100 clothes – me and the two kids (on average)

£300 going out

£45 phone bill

£9.99 Spotify

£5.99 Netflix

Monthly costs: £1460.98

This is what I *need* to earn each month. If I earn less, I will forgo the 'going out' and clothes fund. If I earn a lot more than this, I put a chunk in savings or pay for a holiday or buy something that we need for the house. But in terms of my day rate, if I'm working two days a week, I divide £1460.98 by eight – two days a week, for a month – and get £182.62. That's what I need to earn during the childcare hours. But that doesn't account for time off, tax, savings, equipment, website costs, so initially I doubled it – and a bit more – and set my day rate at £500. But as I've gained experience, I've continued to increase it. I now charge £800 a day. If I then spend a day writing an article for the *Guardian* and I'm only paid £180, I can make up for this by doing a day of consultancy, or offering a company a sponsored post on The Early Hour, and charging £800. It's a balancing act, like everything.

Sali Hughes was a single mum to her two children when they were younger. For Sali, the worst thing about being a freelance mum was – and is – the fear of getting ill and not being able to work for a while. 'Not having sick pay. Not having paid holiday. Always thinking you're losing out on money. It's incredibly difficult; working out what would happen if you suddenly became too ill to work for a period. As a mother, your raison d'être is making sure everything's ticking over. I have savings but it still plays on my mind, and I'm somebody who's in a place in my career with plenty of work and money and all that but there's something about the structure of freelancing that plays into your insecurities as a mother. You can intellectualise it: I know people in staff jobs who don't know whether they'll still have a job next year. But my entire family is wholly reliant on me – I am, too – and that's a lot. And it's something that people have to consider.'

Holly June Smith, a freelance celebrant and coach, says that every freelancer should have an 'emergency fund', which equates to three months' worth of bills, in savings. 'Having that financial buffer has been used for all sorts of things like training, car repairs, flights home for funerals, etc.,' she says. 'There are various reasons why people might need access to a chunk of cash at short notice and most freelancers end up having to put unexpected purchases on credit cards. It's never too early to start squirrelling some cash away. Having my emergency fund meant I was able to take the leap from one sector to another, and it's even more important for freelancers who might choose to take their business in a new direction.'

But what I'm a bigger fan of is Holly's 'fuck it' fund. She always has £200 in savings that she can spend on luxuries – a spa day, lovely products or a new outfit (that she doesn't need). Interestingly, since setting up this fund, Holly says she's not yet touched it. 'The first year of parenting has left little room for frivolities!' she says. 'Rest assured it will be spent one day.'

I like this approach to budgeting: a sensible fund to allow for financially quieter periods, and a fund for treating yourself. As a freelancer, and as a mother, you are rarely told what a great job you're doing. Your kids are unlikely to recognise it, and your clients perhaps won't view you in quite the same way as a full-time employee – you won't have appraisals, for instance. For this reason, you need to recognise your own good work, and reward yourself accordingly.

Lucy Mangan found it hard embarking on motherhood with no financial support to fall back on. 'I really regretted not having any maternity pay or leave,' she says. Following a traumatic birth, she wasn't able to work initially, which brought additional stress to an already difficult period. So she recommends saving as much as you can before giving up a job with benefits. 'You are exposed as a freelancer,' she says. And this can be particularly difficult when you're pitching for work with a demanding baby next to you. Having a buffer while you find your feet as a freelancer can relieve a certain amount of pressure, and allow you to more gradually find the work/parenting balance that suits you and your family.

What will the client pay?

I had a woman come to me recently and ask me if I could write two blogs a week for her. I like her and her business, and was keen for this job. But I made an error. I told her that my day rate was £500 and this would take half a day a week, so I could do the job for £250. She's just starting out so this is a huge amount of money to her. She panicked and said it was way too much and that she'd find someone else. I told her there was room for negotiation, and that if she shared her budget, I'm sure we could find a way to work together – for instance, I could write just one blog post a week, or two shorter ones. But it was too late. I'd lost the job by going in too high. It's advisable to ask what the budget is at the outset. That way, you won't frighten off potential clients by quoting a fee that's too high but also, you might end up being paid more. I was approached by a huge homewares store about being in one of their ad campaigns. Rather than tell them my day rate, I asked their budget and they said: £3000 a day. I was pleased I hadn't gone in too soon with my piddly £500 a day request. The job didn't go ahead, but it reminded me that it's good to hold back, sometimes.

My mum is a trained and experienced counsellor. A piece of advice she often gives me is that you don't always need to answer right away. If a client phones and says: 'I need a campaign created next week. The budget's £1000 and it will take three days,' say to her: 'Thank you very much for thinking of me. I'm going to check a few things and get back to you.' Then put down the phone, look at your diary, check the childcare situation and decide whether you're willing to take a lower day rate for a chunk of work. Once you've decided, make contact with the client and give them your answer. Of course, you might decide you'd like the full £1500 that you'd normally charge, so you can go back and tell them this. At this stage, it's worth working out if you should go in even higher: £1800, so that they can barter you back down to £1300 and then you meet at £1500. Most people like to feel they're getting a bargain, even if you know they're not.

I've had hundreds of emails about sponsored posts on The Early Hour. Often the email will say: I'd like to buy a sponsored post and I'll pay you £50. If I like the look of their website or business, I'll go back and say that I'd be happy to talk more, but that I charge £500 for the sponsored post, and additional fees for social media mentions. If they really are interested, they'll miraculously find the budget. If £50 is as high as they can go, it's not going to work out so that's the end of that.

I now ask for consultancy fees up front. I was fed up with the inevitable chasing that followed each session, and with people cancelling last minute, so I set the condition that a booking will be secured once I've received full payment. Some freelancers request 50 per cent up front, but I don't want to have to chase: if you want me to do the work, you'll need to commit to paying me first. No one, as of yet, has disappeared when I've made this clear. In fact, clients seem pleased that the money bit is then out of the way, and we can get on with the work. It stops people from being flighty and cancelling.

Closing the gender pay gap

*'If you're a woman,
you will earn less than a man.'*

Theresa May, 13 July 2016

In 2017, the median hourly rate for women working full-time was about 9.1 per cent less than the median hourly wage for men. That's £1.32 less per hour.[1] The only way to close this gap is to ask for the same amount as men. So when you're setting your day rate, don't just ask other mothers, or women, who work in the same field as you, freelancing, but ask men, too. And if it's higher, choose to set your rate at the same as theirs. Women are at a disadvantage in the workplace by virtue of their sex, and the hope is that employees will soon realise how pointless this is. But in the meantime, as for what you deserve: it's the same as what a man doing your job gets.

How to ask for money and negotiate a higher fee

When I was pregnant, I was working as a full-time copywriter. I needed to save for maternity leave so decided that I'd like my day rate to go from £150 a day to £250. I was reading Sheryl Sandberg's *Lean In* and felt empowered by her words about how pregnancy doesn't render you useless. Unless it's manual labour, you're as capable in the workplace during pregnancy as you are when not pregnant. So I told my boss that I'd been there for 18 months and would like a higher day rate. She agreed that I was due one, and for the last few months of my employment there, I was on £250 a day.

I have a friend, Cara, who's brilliant at negotiating. She's the youngest of three sisters, with a staunch feminist for a mother. Whenever I talk to Cara about work, she'll tell me about the latest pay rise she's demanded. That might sound like a strong word, but her attitude is: I'm worth more, so you should pay me more. I find this incredibly inspiring; seeing a woman who knows she's good at her job ask for that to be recognised. Guess what? Her bosses always say yes. We've joked that she negotiates 'like a man'. She asks for what she wants, and she gets it. So I often have Cara in mind when I want to negotiate a higher fee. I channel my inner 'Cara' and go for gold. Usually, it works. It's about confidence and knowing your worth, but also gauging the scope beforehand. For a startup, a higher rate might not be possible. For a corporate company, it will be. Do your research, decide on your price, and ask for it.

That said, I was given some valuable advice by life coach Nicky Raby. At the time, I was keen to secure work with a company I loved but I was concerned that as it was a startup they wouldn't be able to afford my rate, or get me on board. Nicky said, 'Don't worry about what they can afford to pay. That's none of your business. Pitch for the work, tell them what you charge, and they'll decide whether it's financially viable.' She was right. I followed her advice, and got the work.

• •

Repeat work

Every freelancer's dream is to get repeat work. This means you can continue to work from home, or your shared workspace, but each week you have the same client(s) paying you to do a specific job. At the moment, I blog for Forbes and BabyCentre each week, and I'm in charge of content for the Clementine app. This is my bread and butter money, and amounts to around £1400 a month. Once I've done these two jobs, my monthly costs are nearly covered. I then only have to secure a couple of articles, or a day of consultancy, and I'm all set. This frees up the remainder of my allotted work days for finding more work, doing some research or working on a project that won't pay immediately – like the novel I'm writing. If you're looking for repeat work, develop a good relationship with all your clients so that they love working with you. Then make suggestions: think of ways you could add value to their business – by creating a weekly role for yourself within their existing framework.

● ●

What does success mean to you?

Success looks different to different people. For me, success means spending lots of time with my kids, working enough to pay my way, having a fairly humble yearly holiday on a French camping site in the summer and perhaps a few weekends at the seaside each year, staying in an Airbnb. I like to look the part, so buying a couple of new items of clothing every few months feels good. We enjoy spending a Saturday afternoon in the pub, with the kids, without having to worry about how much a G&T costs. To someone else, success might mean turning over £1 million a year. Or having 12 weeks off a year.

Steph Douglas, of the blog Don't Buy Her Flowers, says: 'Work out what success is to *you*. Then when you're worried you're going off course or thinking about your next step, you can go back to what success looks like. For me it included being around if the kids need me and being able to take family holidays, so when work takes over I sometimes need to remember why I wanted to run my own business in the first place and that it wasn't just about growing a business as quickly as possible.'

So you decide what success looks like for you and make sure that you don't lose sight of this. If, like Steph, you're keen to take family holidays: ensure you are taking them and not working while you're away. If you're earning all the money but not having enough family time, or not enjoying spending some of it, what's it all for?

● ●

Be realistic

Holly Tucker launched Not on the High Street after having her son, who'd sleep under the kitchen table where she was working. It was all in a bid to create the work–life balance she was after, but that doesn't mean it was easy. She says: 'Building Not on the High Street was so demanding, as was this tiny baby I'd just brought into the world. Both needed my constant attention. Just as things started to go really well, we came to the end of our financial runway. One of the toughest things I had to do was raise investment to pay salaries and keep the lights on, while being a knackered new mum. It was exhausting!'

Remember to cut yourself some slack. Being a mother *is* exhausting and freelance work can be, too. The flexibility you're chasing might appear to be forever out of reach, as you're working your arse off and yet constantly feeling like you're not being a good-enough mum or a good-enough worker. In time, you'll hopefully find a balance that works for you and your family, but there will always be some projects that will have to be turned down if you don't have childcare or you're ill. Try not to feel guilty about this. You're doing the best job you can.

When you're not working, don't be afraid to just chill. Cherry Healey spends her working week making BBC documentaries, often involving lots of travel and time away from her two kids. She found that at the weekends she was then trying to have an amazing social life and host impressive lunches. 'Breakdown is a strong word,' she says, 'but I'd have lots of people over for a BBQ and end up crying on someone's shoulder.' She realised that rather than putting herself under yet more pressure to perform in some way, she just wanted someone else to do the cooking and the cleaning. 'So this weekend,' she says, 'we went to an air-conditioned restaurant for burgers. It's all about going out. Every so often, if I have the energy, I have people over. But every time, I forget how hard it is: we spend a fortune, work our arses off. We'll still be clearing up from Saturday's lunch on Sunday evening. Weekends become sacred when you're working in the week, and your friends will understand if you don't have so much time for them.'

When Cherry told a friend that the mental load was becoming too intense; there was always so much to do and so many people to see, her friend said: 'This is the rush hour of your life. If you're doing a commute at rush hour, do you try to do a spreadsheet?' She had the realisation that it's enough to work, to pay the bills, and then to take it easy with her family – to go out and socialise rather than feeling you have to provide for everyone else all the time.

• •

Official stuff

— **Set up as a sole trader.** This is a government requirement for all self-employed people and will ensure that you're registered and can submit your tax return. More information can be found here: www.gov.uk/set-up-sole-trader.

— **Invoicing.** You'll need to send invoices to your clients once the job is completed. You can find templates online, but the most important information is: date, your name and address, the client's name and address, the invoice number – so for the first job for a new client it will be 01; for the second job for them: 02.

A brief description of the job you've carried out. And your payment terms; for instance, payment within 30 days. You might need to chase them for payment, if you haven't received it within this time frame.

— **Accounting.** I keep a record of all my incomings and outgoings on an excel sheet. Each year, when I'm submitting my self-assessment tax return online (www.gov.uk/self-assessment-tax-returns), this comes in very handy. You can also use software systems like Crunch or Xero that help you to get super organised with your accounting.

— **Tax-deductible expenses.** If you've bought a new computer, or spent money on work-related travel, keep a receipt. This can be logged as work expenses, and you won't have to pay tax on them – the sum total of all your expenses will be deducted from the total amount you've earned and you'll just pay tax on what remains. Working from home, you can also claim a proportion of costs for lighting, heating, cleaning, insurance, mortgage interest, council tax, water rates and general maintenance.[2]

- **30 free hours of childcare.** All children in England are entitled to 570 free hours of childcare per year from an approved childcare provider (childminder or nursery) from the age of three.

- **Tax-Free Childcare.** You can get up to £500 every three months (£2000 a year) for each of your children to help with the costs of childcare. If you get Tax-Free Childcare, the government will pay £2 for every £8 you pay your childcare provider via an online account. You can use it to pay for approved childcare. You can get Tax-Free Childcare at the same time as 30 hours of free childcare if you're eligible for both.[3]

- **Childcare Tax Credit.** The eligibility criteria depends on how many children you have, and the cost of your childcare. But if you're a single parent, working 16+ hours a week; or a couple both working 16+ hours a week and your total household income is under £46,000, it's worth checking what financial support you're entitled to. Some people with a higher household income may still be eligible, especially if you have more than one child, or a disabled child.[4]

And if you or your partner are disabled, you may not both need to work a 16+ hour week to qualify. It should be noted that you cannot get Tax-Free Childcare at the same time as claiming Working Tax Credit, Child Tax Credit, Universal Credit or childcare vouchers. An online calculator – www.gov.uk/childcare-calculator – can help you to work out what will be best for your situation.

— **Disability Living Allowance and Child Tax Credits.** Photographer Penny Wincer has two children, one of whom has special needs. She explains that children with a disability are eligible for DLA (Disability Living Allowance). 'There are three levels of care – low rate, medium rate and high rate. When you have a child on the highest care rating, if you also receive Child Tax Credits, you get a higher rate on those too. The low and medium rates have no effect on other tax credits. DLA is not means-tested, it's to help with the costs of raising a disabled child so it is open for everyone to apply. There is also a low and high rate of mobility that you can claim for. This is for children with mobility issues. My son's

DLA increases my general Child Tax Credits but it doesn't affect the childcare element of the Tax Credits. I get the childcare element simply because I'm a single working parent with two children.'

— **Tax.** You'll have to pay 20 per cent tax on everything you earn above the tax-free allowance of £11,850,[5] up to £46,350. Anything above that will be taxed at 40 per cent. And earnings above £150,000 are taxed at 45 per cent. So for each payment that comes in, make sure you put a decent chunk of it in a separate account. You don't want to be left with a huge tax bill after having spent all your earnings as they've come in.

— **Budgeting.** The app Squirrel allows you to split your salary into bills, savings and a weekly allowance to spend on whatever you like. As a freelancer, you'll then know what you need to earn per working day.

— **Maternity allowance.** Most self-employed women are entitled to maternity allowance, which is currently £140.98 a week. To get the full amount, you must be paying Class 2

National Insurance for at least 13 of the 66 weeks before your baby's due. If you haven't paid the full amount, you'll get £27 a week for 39 weeks. You may be able to get the full amount by making NI payments in lieu or early payments for the following year. More info can be found at www.gov.uk/maternity-allowance/eligibility.

- **KIT days.** Employees and self-employed workers are entitled to 10 keeping in touch (KIT) days during parental leave. This means that you can be paid for work for 10 days during the period you're claiming Maternity Allowance.

3
The daily routine

'People whose performance peaks in the morning are better positioned for career success.'

Christoph Randler, biologist

When my daughter was born, I decided that I'd be relaxed about bedtimes. For the first few months, I kept her up with me until 10 p.m., then we'd settle down for the night together – her in the Moses basket, me in bed with my husband. Throughout the night, she'd wake for feeds and then in the morning, we'd get up together. But soon, it felt as if the umbilical cord was still attached. Because I was breastfeeding her, this was sometimes unavoidable, but when she was around eight weeks old, I introduced a bedtime routine for her. Soon she was going to bed on her own and sleeping for a few hours. Suddenly, I could talk to my husband without a baby hanging off my boob or draped across my chest. It felt liberating.

I quickly realised that babies love routine. In the same way that most adults, at least before having kids, have a good idea of what their working week will entail: waking at a particular time, eating breakfast (or not), leaving the house on time to catch a train or walk to work. Everything is timed – and it works. Most of us thrive on routine. We like to know when we're going to eat, work and sleep – really, it's about survival: we need these things to exist. Babies are the same. And young kids. My daughter loves her Monday–Friday school routine – she knows where she's going, when and for how long. The repetition suits her so much that in the holidays, when timings are looser, she's been known to say: can I go back to school now, please?

As a freelancer, it's important that you have some kind of routine, too. At times, it will feel manic and like you're working non-stop and never have a break. This is hard, but it won't always be like this. I had periods after the birth of my son where I thought I was going mad. My daughter was at nursery two days a week and on the other days, the three of us were muddling through together. Sometimes the kids would nap at the same time and I could work – but not always. I remember days where I'd feel hot in the face and want to scream because my head felt so jammed full of obligations – work, kids, family, friends. I felt very anxious. But once my baby was in more of a routine: at night, and with his day naps, things started to slot into place.

How to start your day

When I set up The Early Hour, the idea was that articles would be published at 5 a.m. for parents who were up early with babies. This meant there was a morning focus to some of the content, and I soon became obsessed with people's morning routines: what time they rose, how they woke up, what they drank first thing (tea, coffee, juice, smoothie, water, hot water and lemon?) and whether they exercised. So I started a series of interviews called My Early Hour, and later: My Morning Routine. I discovered that most people have a very set routine first thing; particularly the successful people. And so I started to implement aspects of these successful people's morning routines into my own.

i. Ban screens in the bedroom

Steph Douglas told me about a trip she'd taken to the Lake District with her family. There was no phone signal or wifi where they were staying and she realised how much better it was to start the day without looking at her phone. 'I'd blame being tired on the kids,' she said, 'and they are pretty tiring, but I found not jumping straight on to emails and social media means you actually sleep more.' She decided to incorporate this into daily life at home, so they bought an alarm clock and now leave their phones downstairs overnight.

Initially, on hearing this, I thought: nahh, not me. I need to have my phone next to me, just in case. But actually, I was already putting it on airplane mode overnight so that I wouldn't have drunken Whats-App messages coming through in the early hours, or the annoying ping of a new email. I decided to follow in Steph's footsteps and leave the phone downstairs overnight, and I'm not exaggerating when I say it revolutionised both my mornings and nights. It meant first thing, I could lie and think rather than grab my phone and check the 'likes' on social media. And before bed, I began reading a novel rather than googling fatal children's illnesses, or where to buy the best dungarees. My dreams even changed; they were no longer infiltrated by the people I'd been looking at on my Instagram feed just before bed.

ii. Exercise first thing

Once up, I get straight into my running clothes. There's something about exercising first thing that works for many freelancers and entrepreneurs; it's like you've achieved something before the day has even begun. And there are also all those lovely endorphins rushing around your body, giving you a big boost. I find my morning run, even if I can only manage five minutes – a quick jaunt around the block – is when I have my best ideas. As soon as I'm out of the door, the ideas start flowing in a way that they don't if I go straight to my desk (or, more accurately, the kitchen table). Also, it feels good to give your body a chance to stretch and wake up, as well as your mind.

However, mornings – particularly in terms of exercise – are always a work-in-progress for me, depending on where I'm at in my life. My pre-children days of long runs and mindfully eaten, wholesome breakfasts are long gone. I now have less time and my priorities have had to change, but also, our routine is constantly evolving. Immediately following the birth of my daughter, I couldn't run so I lay in bed until 8 or 9 a.m., breastfeeding her, and allowing my body to recover. Sometimes, I'd just stand in the garden for five minutes, to wake myself up with some fresh morning air. After six weeks, I started running again – often with the buggy – but bouts of mastitis meant I'd have to take a few weeks off and then start again, slowly.

After my son's birth, I did something stupid. I set myself a challenge to run 13 miles one evening when he was four months old. I was trying to prove that motherhood couldn't slow me down but it hugely backfired, as I ended up having to see an osteopath for six months, who advised me to stop running completely until the damage was rectified. Once my internal lady bits were back in order, I started running again – very short distances – and while I experiment from time to time with longer distances, I usually stick to a 10-minute morning run, stopping halfway round to stretch. I love feeling the air on my face, having 10 minutes to myself first thing and the way I feel once I'm home (and showered).

Arianna Huffington also starts the day with exercise. She co-founded online news and blogging platform The Huffington Post in 2005, working from her kitchen table, and sold it six years later to AOL for $315 million. So if you're basing success on financial terms, Arianna is up there. However, when Huff Post took off, she suffered with ill health due to working long hours and not getting enough sleep. After fainting from exhaustion, Arianna decided she had to make some drastic changes to her lifestyle, so she began to study the importance of sleep, rest, switching off from technology and taking breaks.

iii. Gratitude and intention-setting

Arianna's morning routine is the stuff of legend (if you're as obsessed with mornings and routines as I am): no electronic devices, thoughts of gratitude and intention-setting, 30 minutes of either yoga or on the exercise bike, 30 minutes of meditation, a shower, getting dressed and drinking a Bulletproof coffee. Some parts of her routine vary, depending on where she is. For instance, she explained, 'If I'm travelling and away from my stationary bike, I may have to skip a day. And some days, depending on my schedule, it may be closer to five minutes of meditation. But overall, I keep to my routine – it helps me to centre myself and set my intentions for the day.'

This is something worth bearing in mind, particularly as a mum: it won't always be possible to stick to your routine, so allow for flexibility. But the mental exercises that Arianna practises: intention-setting and practising gratitude, can be easily done wherever you are, and whatever's going on. It's about focusing on what you'd like to achieve that day and being grateful for all the good in your life. Even when things feel terrible, there will be something to be thankful for. Maybe your own good health. Or your family. Or your job. Find it, pause and reflect on it. This will subtly set you up for a day with more of the good stuff. Instead of checking my phone first thing, I try to remember to list three things in my life that I'm grateful for. I'm sure it impacts my mood for at least the early part of the day.

My husband used to hate his job. The company was unsupportive and didn't pay him enough, so every morning, he dreaded having to get out of bed and go to work, and he'd sing: 'gotta get up, gotta get up, gotta get up; don't wanna get up, don't wanna get up, don't wanna get up.' It's probably not a great way to start the day but it was just a reflection of how he felt (he's since changed careers and is much perkier in the mornings). I was keen to know if hugely successful, motivated people like Arianna Huffington sometimes feel similarly unmotivated first thing in the morning, so I asked if she ever lies in bed, thinking, I can't be bothered to get up. Rather than giving tips for meditating your way out of these thoughts, or a herbal tea that will perk you up, she simply answered, 'I think we all have that thought!' I found that quite reassuring.

iv. What time should you get up in the morning?

I went through a period of rising at 5.30 a.m., Monday–Friday, so that I could work before my daughter woke up. Mornings are when I feel most productive, so it made sense for me to go to bed early and rise early, too. I'd use this time to write and reflect. For working parents with no formal childcare arrangement, these early hours are invaluable. They are often the only guaranteed hours you'll have without a baby or toddler demanding your time.

Candice Brathwaite – writer, presenter and co-founder of Make Motherhood Diverse – makes good use of the early morning. She starts her day at 4.30 a.m., as this is when her husband gets up for work. She's a light sleeper so gets up too and uses the time to journal, write her to-do list, work (she's currently writing her first book) and then wait for her four-year-old daughter, Esme-Olivia, to wake up.

If you can muster the energy to slide out of bed before the kids, having some alone-time before the chaos begins can be so beneficial. My second-born, for the first year of his life, was an early riser – he was always up at 6 a.m., sometimes earlier, so I didn't have the opportunity to rise before him and I missed those quiet early morning hours. I'm starting to slowly claw them back, now, as he and his sister sleep until around 7 a.m. I go downstairs, lay out the breakfast bits and work until the rest of the house wakes up. I cherish that time.

v. More planning, less chaos

In my home, once everyone's up, chaos quickly ensues: unprovoked tantrums, Weetabix being thrown across the kitchen, demands for various sweet foods that they aren't allowed in the morning. One strategy I have for reducing the inevitable stress that comes with having young children is to put out their clothes for the next day before they go to bed. I found this particularly helpful in the early months with my son, when I was exhausted and overwhelmed. He was waking up at 4.30 a.m. some mornings, and wouldn't go back to sleep until we were downstairs and he was in his buggy, being rocked. This resulted in me drinking far too much coffee and developing rather acute anxiety. I needed any shortcuts I could find, and laying out tomorrow's outfit was one of them.

So even now, as soon as the kids are up, we get them dressed in those clothes. It means no hanging out in the pjs over breakfast, but I'm willing to forgo that aspect of our mornings for an easier life. My daughter, aged four, has very clear ideas on how she likes to dress so I let her choose and lay out her own clothes. This means one less battle for me in the morning. My son doesn't care what he's wearing but I've developed (this might sound excessive, but it really helps) a colour palette for his clothes. He suits earthy hues, so I only buy clothes in those colours, and ask everyone else to as well. This way, everything matches everything.

I've developed something of a capsule wardrobe for myself, too. I worked out which colours suit me – pastels, cream, light grey, denim – and mostly buy clothes in these shades. That way, I can pull out any top and trousers and get ready really quickly. But I'm also a big fan of brightly coloured dungarees – a whole outfit in one. Plus, putting on bright, patterned clothes always lifts my spirits. I asked Arianna Huffington how she chooses her clothes each day and she said: 'I'm a big believer in repeats. It's one of my missions to make repeats cool! It would save women so much time and energy – which would mean more time and energy they can spend getting things done. Or sleeping.' She said the idea that we need to wear something new every day, while men like Mark Zuckerberg can wear the same hoodie and jeans, is potentially holding us back. She's right.

vi. White teeth

Another way to save time in the morning is by having a second set of toothbrushes and toothpaste in the kitchen. This is a simple but incredibly useful parenting hack. No last-minute dash to the bathroom: eat breakfast, clean teeth, go. And talking of teeth, I picked up a tip from Jasmine Hemsley – celebrity chef, wellbeing expert and author – with whom I was on a panel at *Stylist* Live, discussing the 'Morning Routines of Successful Women'. She incorporates Ayurvedic principles into her everyday life and work, and one of them is tongue-scraping. Bear with me – it sounds gross but this ancient practice, of dragging a bent, copper tongue-scraper over your tongue, really does work. It removes all the food and bacteria that settles there over the day or through the night, and leaves you feeling so fresh in the mouth. They're cheap, too, I got one off Amazon for £3.49. Money well spent.

vii. Breakfast

Some people love it, others have to force themselves to eat first thing and the third group skip it altogether. I straddle all three. I love the food we tend to eat for breakfast in the UK: fresh fruit, cereals, toast. But I don't want to eat as soon as I wake up. So I have two coffees – 'premium instant', Nescafe Azera: quick, creamy, strong – then wait a few hours before eating. If I'm up at 6 a.m., I'll usually have breakfast at 9 a.m., by which time I'll be really hungry. I'll go for granola or All Bran with almond milk, a tablespoon of yoghurt, a dollop of Pip & Nut peanut butter, chia and linseeds (for protein), berries and pear. It keeps me full until lunch. But I'm no chef so check out Anna Jones' quick, healthy breakfast ideas on her website: annajones.co.uk/recipe/meals/breakfast.

Quick tips for your morning routine:

— **Exercise.** If you can't leave the house to go for a run, do 10 minutes of stretching in your sitting room. Then stand in the garden or out the front for a few minutes, breathing in the air.

— **Intention-setting:** think about what you'd like to achieve today. It's a positive start to the day.

- **Gratitude.** Being thankful for all the good in your life will make you feel a lot more upbeat than mentally listing the bad.

- **Tongue-scraping.** Do this when you clean your teeth. You won't look back.

- **Early rising.** Get up before the kids, if possible, and have some time to yourself.

- **Ban phones.** Get an alarm clock and leave your phone downstairs overnight. You'll be amazed at how much better you feel waking up without a bleeping phone next to you.

- **Breakfast.** Wait until you're hungry then enjoy something healthy but filling. It will prevent you grabbing a mid-morning chocolate croissant.

• •

The working day

Each day, it's helpful to plan exactly what you'll be working on. This way, you can focus on those specific tasks and feel a sense of achievement once they're completed. As a freelancing mum, you'll probably have a seemingly neverending 'to-do' list, but the app Wunderlist can help with organisation. Use it to keep track of all your 'to-dos' and sign your partner up, too, so you can share the domestic duties on there. If the list is feeling daunting, tackle the tasks you're least looking forward to first, leaving the rest of your time free for the stuff that excites you. At Propercorn HQ, founder Cassandra Stavrou has implemented a tradition of starting the day with a fake frog placed on each of her employees' desks. This represents the one, niggling task that needs doing but that you're dreading. The idea is that you do that one task, first thing – you 'swallow the frog' – then you can remove the literal or metaphorical frog from your desk and move on.

Sarah Turner says: 'Freelance works best for me when I set myself a task list and schedule for the coming week, i.e. Monday is writing an article for X, Tuesday is clearing emails followed by a meeting with a PR company, Wednesday is book promotion and so on. As I don't have a boss breathing down my neck, I find it important to set myself goals so that I'm able to keep check on whether I am on target or not. Of course, I could then just move those targets, but I find I tend to feel guilty if I haven't achieved what I set out to achieve on my Things to Do list for the week, so I intend to keep writing those lists for motivation!'

Stylist Bertie Bowen is also a fan of routine. 'I do a day job three days a week (freelance, but it is regular, guaranteed work) plus have a blog, extra styling work and writing commitments to fit in around that,' she says. 'I found the best way to stay motivated with the extra stuff was to have a routine and stick to it without thinking about it. I put the kids to bed at 7 p.m. and while my husband cooks (or if he's at work, while my dinner is in the oven) and before I collapse on the sofa, I sit in the kitchen with a big glass of wine and write or research. It could be for half an hour or two hours – depends how tired I am and if I have a deadline. It's the routine which makes me do it. Even if I'm not in the mood, I don't give myself the option not to.'

Lucy Mangan works seven days a week, and 'probably 360 days a year', but in terms of what she's working on, every week is different. However, her weekly *Stylist* column is always written on a Tuesday, so that's become a non-negotiable work day for her. 'Beyond that,' she says, 'I write one TV review a week for the *Guardian*, and then I have short-term commissions. So I might write one to three articles a week, on top of my column and review.' Her new role as the *Guardian*'s lead TV reviewer will mean upping her reviews to four a week, so this will require a new routine: 'It will be like a regular, full-time job,' she says. When she has a day with no journalism commissions, she'll write whichever book she's currently working on. As a freelancer, your routine might be ever evolving, like Lucy's.

i. Dress like you mean business

Whether you're staying at home and working in front of a computer or meeting a client, get your gear on. There's this idea that working from home is amazing because you can wear your pjs all day. Not true. 1, If you have kids in childcare, you can't. You need to get dressed to drop them off or greet the childminder; and 2, It's actually not that amazing slobbing around in your nightwear in the daylight hours. Dressing like you're still in bed will make you *feel* like you're still in bed.

We know that first impressions – in terms of how we present ourselves to other people – are incredibly important, and made quickly. Psychologically, what you see when you look in the mirror matters, too. If you see someone dressed for success: in a considered outfit, hair neatened – this will inspire productivity. Conversely, if you see pyjamas, and someone who isn't ready to face the world, this might instil the notion that she (read: you) isn't ready to start work.

Freelance stylist and mum-of-two Yvadney Davis says: 'Dress for work. Rolling out of bed and onto the laptop is so easy to do, but you have to be intentional when you work from home and dress like at any time a potential client could Skype you. It affects how you approach your work. I for one can be known to sit at my desk wearing my sequin Miu Mius while prepping for a photoshoot.'

ii. Divide the day into chunks

Depending on the amount of time you have to work, you might like to divide it into one-hour chunks – if you have the whole morning – or even smaller; 15-minute chunks, if your child is at nursery for two hours in the morning. You could spend a quarter of an hour on emails, then on planning or writing a blog post, 15 minutes on social media and the next 15 making an important phone call. If, like me, you find it hard to stick to time frames for each exercise, it might work to actually leave the 'frog' until last. If I want to work on my book but have to allocate three hours to working for a client, I often leave the client work until last, as I know that doing it first thing means it'll stay on my mind and feed into the rest of my work hours. Try both and see which method you prefer.

Kelly Seymour – silversmith, jewellery designer and founder of Cult of Youth – divides the day and night into two distinct chunks and works one or the other. 'Try to prioritise every part of your life but in slots you can manage,' she says. 'E.g. If I needed to work and so Elvis watches CBeebies all day then I'd make sure we have a date night eating mac and cheese and putting stickers on each other's face. If we go out all day, the evenings are my work time.'

iii. Take breaks

If you're working the whole day, make time for a proper lunch. Eat filling and healthy food and try to stop working while you eat. I'm not always able to do this, sometimes the window to work is too small, but if I have time, I try to focus on my food, taste it and eat mindfully. It helps me to listen to my body and appetite and will lessen the urge for biscuit-grabbing at regular intervals. On that note, don't stock biscuits in the house, because if you're anything like me, this is such a great procrastination exercise: find biscuits, eat biscuits. When I was in my twenties, I was living in Somerset and working from home. I kept putting on weight so I went to the doctors to ask if I was ill. He said, do you work from home? Yes. Do you eat lots of biscuits? Yes. Mystery solved.

As a mum, the likelihood is that your nights will be disturbed at least for a while. If you feel tired and can't concentrate, try taking a power nap – perhaps when your baby's sleeping. Some of the most success-ful people are big fans of a power nap, a 20-minute rest to restore your energy. Margaret Thatcher famously survived on just four hours' sleep a night, but that's because she took power naps. As did Elea-nor Roosevelt. According to hypnotherapist Georgia Foster, the voice of Clementine app – helping women to feel calmer and sleep better – taking time out of a busy working day will lead to more productivity. 'Power naps rest the conscious mind,' she says, 'but the deeper part of your mind – the problem-solving, idea-generating part of your mind – is always awake.' Even when you're sleeping. So you might wake up with a solution to a challenge that was frustrating you earlier in the day.

Tips for power napping (from Kim Palmer, founder of Clementine app):

— **Get comfy** but not too comfy – sit on the sofa with your headphones in or lie on top of the bed. Don't put your pjs on, as it will signal to your body that you're going into a deep sleep.

— To power-charge your power nap, **have a coffee beforehand.** You'll have double the energy when you wake up.

— Be mindful that **you aren't actually going into a deep sleep** . . . that's kind of the point. Don't sleep for longer than 30 minutes (use an alarm).

— Always **have a glass of water afterwards** to help you feel refreshed and renewed.

On the importance of taking time out, Steph Douglas says: 'No one is going to say: "Ok, you're done, have a break". The only person that can do that is you, so I've learned that sometimes I need to stop and reflect on all the things I *have* achieved rather than focusing on all the things still to do, because when you're running your own business that list will never be finished. If you don't learn when to stop, you'll burn out eventually.'

Eirlie Chisholm runs a kids' clothing brand, free-lances as a pattern cutter and is raising two young boys on her own. What's difficult, she says, is that there is no second income to fall back on. But she still makes sure that when she's finding it all too much, she doesn't push herself to continue working, as it can be counter-productive. 'It ends in wasted time and energy,' she says, 'and I often have to go over things I've done and amend. At times like that I acknowledge it in myself, and visualise myself literally taking a step back. I pause and then go and do something not work-related, either go to a nice café and get a take-away so I can walk around and be really present (no phone) or I treat myself to a middle-of-the-day bath.'

Psychologist Dr Jessamy Hibberd makes sure to allow time for herself. 'It's really important to me that I look after myself,' she says. 'This is something I found harder when I first started. I try not to rush and to make time for the things I enjoy. For me, it's the little everyday things that make all the difference when it comes to taking care of our minds and looking after ourselves and it's these simple everyday things that can make a huge difference to your mental health. My motto is that *what you do every day is what makes the biggest difference.*

Here's what Dr Jessamy Hibberd does each day . . .

- **Gratitude is my favourite strategy.** I love how it turns around the way you perceive your life in such a simple way, and it has huge health benefits.

- **I love a project or goal;** I like having something to focus on and work towards. It gives me a sense of purpose and fulfilment and it's good to do things that mean you step out of your comfort zone.

- **Taking a step back,** slowing down and remembering there's more than one way to look at things is helpful when things feel a bit much.

- For me, **exercise is a big one** – I find it an amazing stress relief. Running gives me time to think and put my thoughts in order and I love the high! I particularly like Park Run, it's such a lovely event – just being part of it makes you feel good.

- **I love my sleep** – when I'm tired I find everything harder. A good night's sleep (when possible!) makes all the difference.

- **Family and friends are really important,** as a source of support, fun and advice.

- **Time outdoors** always makes me feel better, especially with the kids – whether it's the park, beach, bike ride or a walk.

- I also have a saying: **'Always reserve the right to change your mind'**. If something's not working, it lets me look at it and make a change if I need to.

iv. Knowing when to stop work

It can be hard to switch off when you're already squeezing work into tiny pockets when your child is sleeping. However, it's not sustainable to look after kids non-stop all day and then work non-stop all night. Kelly Seymour recommends doing what you NEED to do before you sit down, and leaving the less-important stuff for another time. 'You never really enjoy downtime if you've got things hanging over your head,' she says. She believes that 'done is better than perfect. Worry about things for too long and the moment passes, you lose opportunities,' she says. But if you're easily distracted at the end of the day by the TV in the corner of the room, hide it from view.

Kelly also suggests setting up a work station, even if it's just a corner of a room or a particular section of the sofa. When you're at your station, you're working. But when you've decided to finish work, you remove yourself from that space. 'Squirrel a corner away,' she says. 'If you are like me and a clear space means a clear head (I can't concentrate if everything is a tip), having a space in your home to transform into a work corner – enabling you to turn your back to whatever is going on behind it – is a real asset. I have worked from my sofa for the best part of two years but have just ordered a desk to squeeze into my living room. It will [*will*, she says] stay beautifully clear, no toy cars, no empty coffee cups, no endless receipts – and it will be an oasis in our tiny one-bed flat when everything else is chaos.'

v. Business calls with the kids at your feet

When my son was a few months old, and my daughter was two, Alexis Kingsbury asked me if I'd do an interview for the Parentpreneur Accelerator podcast. It would be conducted over the phone so didn't require any travel, and the focus of our chat was going to be parenting while raising children, so I thought: it will be fine! I'll pop my daughter in front of the telly, my son on the boob and we'll have a brilliant chat! Only, my potty-training daughter suddenly needed a poo and my usually-appeased-by-the-breast son wasn't interested in continuous breastfeeding and started crying. A lot. I was utterly distracted, couldn't think of anything interesting to say and the interview involved a lot of shouting over children. Needless to say, Alexis couldn't use it. In fact, before he had the chance to tell me how terrible it had been, I asked if we could do it again. This time, I asked my mum to come and watch the kids while I walked around the block, away from distractions, talking into my headphones. I was able to remember all the points I'd planned, and deliver them fairly articulately. A far cry from the jumbled, frantic utterings of our previous Skype call.

If you have a business call to make or receive, a Skype interview, a pitch, a journalist interviewing you about your work, plan it for a time in the day when you don't have the kids. That might be the evening, once they're in bed, or during nap-time – if this is reliable – or when you have childcare or can draft in a friend or family member to watch them for an hour. You need to be able to focus on the conversation and when you're looking after your child(ren) there's no guarantee of this being possible. I know one woman who put her child down for a nap, made the important business call and then her daughter woke up. She left her in the cot, shouting, for 20 minutes while she finished the call. And felt terrible afterwards. But this is the kind of challenge you will face as a freelance mum: finish the call as soon as your child wakes, or leave them in what you know to be a safe space while you finish the business chat as soon as you can without losing the client.

vi. 'Working from home'

You might find that friends think because you work from home, you're not really working. This can become very frustrating, especially if they can't understand why you're not available to meet for a coffee or have them round. Sometimes I feel incredibly inflexible, as I can only offer two- or three-hour time slots to meet people – between naps, meals, working and in the evenings. But it's the only way I can get enough done. It can be useful to set clear boundaries, with friends and family, like: on Mondays, Tuesdays and Wednesdays I'm keeping the diary clear so that I can work when the baby sleeps. They should understand that this means you don't want unexpected visitors on these days. If you fancy socialising on the days you haven't allocated for working but no one you know is free, there are apps like Peanut and Mush that connect you with mothers in your area who are also looking for company. After all, the freelance mum life – working unsociable hours – can get lonely.

Lisa Williams, freelance journalist and digital consultant, says: 'If you work from home, make sure you don't isolate yourself. While it has its benefits (getting the laundry done during your tea breaks and not having to put on any makeup), it can be excruciatingly lonely, which in turn can fuel anxiety and catastrophising. If any friends are freelance, take turns to host work sessions so you have someone to bounce ideas off and talk Netflix while you have lunch. Do it even if they're not in the same sector as you; it's amazing what an outsider's perspective can do for you when you're facing a dilemma.'

There may also be a grey area when it comes to work meetings – you might be asked to meet with someone, only to realise half the day's gone and you've come away with nothing. Anniki Sommerville – author, co-founder of The Hotbed Collective website and podcast, and editor of Selfish Mother blog – says she sometimes gets annoyed about people reaching out and wanting to have coffee or a catch-up. 'I can't afford to just have chats willy nilly to see what might come out of it. I find all of that hard to navigate and sometimes a waste of time, unsure whether it's about cultivating a friendship or a useful business connection. I only have two clear days a week so that time needs to be profitable and doesn't leave much time to "hang out".' She suggests being clear on why you're meeting up with that person. Is it to be seen with certain people? Is it to raise your profile? Is it to socialise with people you like? Or is it work?

Sali Hughes says that if you're someone who 'goes to work' it can be easier to separate home and work. 'Sometimes my physical presence at home suggests I'm here, and Mum, but actually I'm at work, writing.' It's especially hard when they're young, she says, and so establishing structure, though difficult when you have babies, is necessary. 'Having some kind of shape to the day can be beneficial – working during nap-times, or when they're at nursery. You have to be quite disciplined to have a structure, which comes naturally in an office.'

Kelly Seymour says: 'Make time for no one and nothing but you. This is hard when you run a business via social media which is 24/7 and are a solo parent, because there's no one to pick up the slack when you've got nothing left or your head is frazzled after a day of negotiating with a toddler and you need to locate an order that last got traced in Sydney . . . BUT one morning of nursery time a week, I go to the gym. I'm no good if my head isn't. My brain doesn't work and therefore I don't work productively. Making space for me to exist outside of being needed in different ways is not just important but vital.'

vii. Cleaning: do it, don't do it or hire help

When at home, working, there are plenty of potential distractions – not just your children. The cleaning, for instance. These days, I don't put clothes in the washing machine on my working days, because it means I'll have to put away the dry clothes and hang out the wet ones. When my son was newborn, and I didn't have the time or the energy to do regular whole-house cleans, I used the app Bizzby to get a cleaner once a week. You book and pay online, no money changes hands. Now I do it myself while my son follows me around pretending to dust. The house is never immaculate, but it's good enough. I have big baskets in the kitchen and living room that I can throw all the toys into so it's more of a room 'sweep' than having to organise anything properly.

If you're an obsessive clearer, like me, life coach Nicky Raby recommends tackling the 'chaos' – food on the floor and up the walls, clutter – 15 minutes before bathtime. This means that once the kids' bedtime routine is done you can come down, or into, a calmer and clearer space, which is particularly beneficial if you're going to be working in the evening.

Candice Brathwaite says: 'My working-class upbringing isn't yet completely comfortable with paying for a cleaner, etc., but I've come to find it's the only way to free up time for things that pay me/I enjoy (luckily those two things are the same now!).' Sometimes, it's about outsourcing where you can so that you can focus on the work you want to be doing rather than the chores you feel obliged to be doing. Also, it will probably work out cheaper to pay someone to do a few hours' cleaning and to spend those hours working on your freelance career.

viii. Saying no

When you're starting out as a freelancer, it can be really tough to say no to work. Until you've established a name for yourself, and have loads of clients and there's money coming in, you'll probably say 'yes' to everything and find a way to do it. However, you don't want to end up resenting both work and family life (I've been there; it sucks). So once you're on the right track, start thinking about saying 'no' from time to time. If the job will earn you lots of money but make home life stressful, or take you away from the kids at an important time – as they start school, for example – turn it down. Even better: pass it on. This will make your client happy, as well as your freelance pal who's getting the extra work. Hopefully, they'll do the same when they're in a similar position.

A while back, I was working with a freelance journalist on a project. She has three kids and was finding things tough. The *Guardian* asked her to write an opinion piece and she was torn. She wanted the work, but didn't know anything (or care) about the news story it was in response to, and she was already really busy. She reluctantly turned down the work. Sometimes, it's not worth the stress. Zoë de Pass, founder of Dress Like a Mum, says: 'Don't take on too much and don't be afraid to say no to things. Ultimately, nothing is more important than life, love and health, so being realistic about what can and can't be achieved is important.' I'm inclined to agree.

Also, be mindful of how long you spend engaging with requests. As you become an expert in your field, people will want favours from you. As a 'people pleaser', I find it very hard to say no, but I've had to learn how to filter through the requests. If someone asks me for advice and I have a spare 10 minutes, and I like the person, I'll do it. If I'm rushing or don't get great vibes, I'll tell them I'm too busy. I often find myself in the middle of a project when an email comes in saying: 'Can you just watch this film I've made, it's really short, and tell me what you think?', or 'Would you mind reading through this?' My inclination is to help out but I have to stop myself, tell them I'm busy and either add it to my list to come back to or explain that I won't be able to help this time. It's about managing expectations.

My friend Danielle Pender, editor of *Riposte Magazine*, only responds to emails that are relevant to her and/or her work. Since hearing this, I've really taken stock of how much time I spend responding to emails from people I don't know, won't be working with and won't gain anything from. This might sound harsh, but time is precious. I don't want to spend even five minutes explaining to a PR why I won't be including their client's product in a round-up on The Early Hour (though, if you're interested, it's because I don't do 'round-ups' or product reviews). When I launched The Early Hour, I was keen to develop relationships with everyone but now I only reply to an email if it's mutually beneficial, or if I actually wanted to help the other person. It's about prioritising you, your family and your career.

Sometimes you'll desperately want to say yes but it just won't work out. I was recently invited to a training day at Apple HQ. I have a secret obsession with these massive tech companies – Apple, Facebook, Google – and would love a nose around, some free doughnuts and to hear their innovative thoughts on the tech world. But I couldn't get the childcare for my son. I've used a babysitting app, Bubble, when my daughter's at home too, as I know she'll look out for her brother, but I didn't want him to be alone with someone he'd never met before. So, after much umming and ahh-ing, I admitted defeat and said: thank you, but I can't come. A missed opportunity, but one that might come along again.

Cherry Healey makes documentaries for the BBC three/four days a week. 'I have more money when I work four days,' she says, 'but I have kids so sometimes I say no to work. It's not ideal, as I'm running a house of four people on a part-time salary [they have a live-in au pair]. Also, because I work for the BBC I have to say no to lots of branding work. But then the more I work, the more stressful it all is. If I do four days a week, I only really see the kids on the weekend. Sometimes it balances just fine, sometimes we're living on the edge. If you're on the telly, it doesn't necessarily mean you're earning good money. And I have a big group of people to support.' So saying 'no' is about protecting family time, protecting your sanity and adjusting the balance.

Sali Hughes says she won't ever miss a school concert, whatever the job is. 'I'm determined to the point that an Addison Lee once collected me from the school gates, after a concert, to take me to Gatwick to fly to New York. We spend too much time pretending we can do everything – and it's not helpful: for you, for companies. Or for other women with perhaps less power. So I will always say: "I'm not doing that, because . . ." It's taken quite a few years to get to a position where I can say that. And I likewise wouldn't hesitate to cancel dinner or a meeting if my son was sent home from school or bumped his head (these are things that have actually happened). Some people don't get it and it's an opportunity to educate them. My son was extremely ill in hospital and it was very telling which of my employers said: don't you dare do any work (like the *Guardian* and *The Pool*), and those who phoned me every day asking if I'd finished my work. One client wanted me to film a test shot from hospital. I said no.'

ix. Teatime

Unless you have a childminder or nanny who is cooking your children's tea, this is something you'll have to factor into your day. I sometimes find myself panic-buying freezer food and whacking it in the oven when I'm strapped for time, but what makes me feel much better is doing just a little bit of forward planning. So

I might buy a load of veg and some chopped tomatoes in the morning, after dropping my daughter, then I'll chop everything up after my son's afternoon nap, just before heading out to collect my daughter. When we get home, they play or watch TV and I whack it all in a pan, add the chopped tomatoes, some beans and spices and call it a chilli. We all eat together at 5 p.m.

However, Claire Thomson – the 5 O'Clock Apron, an author and former *Guardian* columnist – creates lovely, inspired family dinner recipes. I asked her how she finds the time and she said: 'I want to cook only the one meal when the kids come home from school. It's important to me that we all eat the same supper sitting together at the kitchen table, it's an important juncture in the day. I started my Instagram feed (@5oclockapron) to demonstrate to other working parents that good wholesome suppers were achievable in a practical timeframe. I cook with an eye for sustenance, budget and always flavour.

'Recipes like braised lentils, beans, soups or workhorse tomato pasta sauces freeze brilliantly and give much-needed back-up should time be of the essence when you get home and the kids are clamouring but you don't want them filling up on snacks. I especially love the cheap versatility of ingredients like gram flour – mixed speedily with a measure of water and a good pinch of turmeric and garam in a jug, as you dash about in the morning, it makes a batter you can just let sit there on the worktop as the day unfolds, until you get home and are ready to cook. Fried into thin pancakes and served with yogurt and jarred pickles, this is a supper that takes five minutes to assemble.'

● ●

The baby's bedtime routine and daytime naps

When my daughter was a few months old, I started to crave some time alone – and with my husband, so I started a bedtime routine: bath, milk, bed. She soon understood that after the bath, she'd be settling down for a feed and then heading into her Moses basket. Some nights, she'd only stay asleep a couple of hours, others a little longer. But I began to have at least the early part of the evening to myself. So when my son was born, we started this same routine at around the four-week mark. The first night, he slept an hour then needed another feed. But the next night, he slept maybe two hours. Soon he was having a good stretch of sleep between 7 p.m. and midnight.

As I said earlier, babies love the familiarity of routines. And once they're able to tell that it's bedtime and now they'll be having a good kip before waking for the first night-feed, you can potentially spend this time doing some brainstorming or planning, connecting with people on Instagram, retweeting on Twitter. Anything that feels doable in your probably quite tired state. Or just kick back and watch a good BBC drama and start the evening work when they're a little bit older. Either way, establishing this bedtime routine will free you up if you're hankering after some alone time in the evenings.

i. Night-time routine

I spoke to Kerry Secker, a baby sleep consultant, about how to get my son into a good night-time sleeping routine and she explained that for the first three months, baby sleep will be quite unreliable. They may sleep for longer stretches of four hours but this could then be followed by a 15-minute cat nap. And this can happen day and night. Most babies take about 12 weeks to regulate their melatonin production (the sleep hormone), and to sort out the difference between day and night. This is all about the circadian rhythm – the physiological changes that follow a 24-hour cycle (awake in daylight hours, asleep at night – when it's dark).

From six months old, babies have a set schedule in terms of melatonin production. From around 3 p.m. each day, they start to produce melatonin. It gradually rises, peaks at 7 p.m. and stays consistent until midnight, so this is the deepest part of their sleep. If your baby wakes before midnight, it shouldn't be so hard to resettle them; this is why getting them to have a good chunk of sleep in the earlier part of the evening tends to be easier.

For the baby's night-time routine, Kerry says you should keep it short and sweet. Dinner, bath (no more than 10 minutes), a book in the room they sleep in then say goodnight to three objects in the room – like the window, the door and the bookshelves. This is an additional part of the routine that will signal to your baby that soon it's lights out and time for sleep. It's a nice way of making their room feel cosy and familiar each night before bed (whether they're in your bedroom, or their own).

ii. Napping in the daytime

Once your baby moves out of the newborn phase it can be a bit of a shock, as they might suddenly need a lot more stimulation and entertaining: time outdoors, rattle-shaking, playing with teddies. It's at this stage that the naps can become golden: it's your chance to have a break, which you can use for your work or to just catch up on sleep. Either way, it's invaluable downtime. So, how to get your baby to nap?

First, you need some idea of how much sleep your baby should be having. The table opposite documents approximate day- and night-time sleep durations, by age.

Getting your baby to nap during the day is much the same as at night: establish a routine. With both my two, I spent the first few months rocking them to sleep in the buggy. Some 'sleep experts' advise against this, but I ignored them and it worked for us, both times. I'd take them for a walk around the block and once they dropped off, return home and have a little rest on the sofa while they snoozed. Around the four-month mark, I started leaving them in the cot for a morning nap – around two hours after waking – then an afternoon nap, about three hours after they'd

Age	Daytime sleep	Night-time sleep	Total sleep
Newborn	8 hours (3 naps)	8 hours and 30 minutes	16 hours and 30 minutes
One month	6–7 hours (3 naps)	8–9 hours	14–16 hours
Three months	4–5 hours (3 naps)	10–11 hours	14–16 hours
Six months	3 hours (3 naps)	11 hours	14 hours
Nine months	2 hours and 30 minutes (2 naps)	11 hours	13 hours and 30 minutes
12 months	2 hours and 30 minutes (2 naps)	11 hours	13 hours and 30 minutes
18 months	2 hours (1 nap)	12 hours	12–14 hours

woken from the morning nap. Both became fairly proficient nappers so that by the time they were six months old, I'd have a one-and-a-half- to two-hour window in the morning, and the same in the afternoon, when they were asleep and I could work.

I'm not a sleep expert, although the amount of research (googling) I've done makes me feel like I am sometimes, and every baby's different – some simply won't nap. But what worked for me to get them napping in the cot was having the curtains closed, it being quiet (an industrial white noise machine on at full blast when my neighbours started their house renovations), and ensuring they had tummies full of milk. Also, I put a sign on the front door saying: 'Please do not knock on the door, my baby's napping. Knock gently on the sitting-room window instead. Thanks!' Everyone on my street thought I was an idiot but they probably didn't realise this was the only time I had to properly work. Soon, the delivery people became very good at the window-tap. And it meant the baby never woke up unnecessarily. But you'll work out your own routine (via Google, probably). And once you do, you'll be extremely grateful for this time.

Your night-time routine

The time you go to bed, whether you hit the booze or drink water, and your last waking thought will all have an impact on how you feel first thing in the morning. In *Why We Sleep*, the first ever in-depth study into sleep, the author Matthew Walker explains that we need eight hours' sleep a night to stave off serious mental and physical illnesses. This can fill new parents with panic, as it's not always possible to clock up eight hours at night, but if you at least ensure the sleep you do have is restful, that's a good start. So, like my morning routine, I now pay close attention to how I wind down at the end of the day, taking tips from women around me who seem to have it all sussed in order to refine my before-bed routine and get the optimum amount of sleep.

i. Bedtime

With two young children who might wake in the night for a feed (the one-year-old), or the toilet (the older one), it's trickier to get those eight hours of nod. They are up most mornings by 6 a.m., so in order to get my eight hours, I need to go to bed by

10 p.m. Well, I need to be asleep then. And to account for any night-wakings, nearer 9 p.m. is even better. When I first realised that I needed to go to bed way earlier than I was (back then: 11–12 p.m.), I felt a bit down. 'I won't have a life!' I said to my husband. 'You already don't have a life,' he replied. And he was right. We don't. Well, not like the sociable days of old. I actually love my more sober, rave-free life. However, when telling people what time I go to bed their faces say it all: boring mum. So yes, that's what I've become. But d'you know what? I feel pretty good for it.

So after eating with the kids at 5.30 p.m., we run a bath with only hot water. I get in for a cheeky dip, just for a few minutes, and then we add water and the kids join me. By 6.30 p.m., we're all in our pyjamas. (Yeah, 'sad mum', but it's more comfortable than my day clothes and saves time later on when I'm exhausted and want to dive straight into bed.) We each take one child and do stories then tuck them in. They're asleep by 7 p.m.

Most evenings, I end up working on my laptop. Occasionally, I'll need a break so I will watch a film or TV drama. I decided that as I was mostly forgoing nights out for the time being, I'd stop drinking booze midweek. Being sober means I can go to bed even earlier and read a novel. Some evenings, I'll head up at 8.30 p.m., planning on reading until 10 p.m. But a few pages in, I'll feel myself drifting off. And so, reader, I'll tell you the truth: sometimes it's lights out before 9 p.m. But I'll wake up the next morning feeling tiptop and that's important whether it's a working day or a mothering day, as both require heaps of energy. While writing this book, bedtime has sometimes crept to past 11 p.m. but this means if I have a disturbed night with my son, because he's ill, the next day's a write-off. Literally.

The kid-friendly night-time routine has stolen my social life but bestowed me with more energy, positivity and focus in the daytime. And right now, while the kids are young, that's what I need most: bearable days, not wild nights out. Even a midweek dinner with friends can throw me into a mini panic, as I know I'll pay for it the next day. As a freelancer, I don't have the option of sitting at my desk and not doing much work: if I don't get it done, I don't get paid. So I keep nights out to a minimum and try to meet people at the weekends instead. Though I do love the occasional solo trip to the cinema: a great way to avoid getting a babysitter or having to fit in with other people. If you're solo-parenting, a baby-sitting swap might work.

ii. Sali Hughes' wind-down routine

Sali Hughes is a night owl; she does a lot of her best work in the evening. Her first book was mostly written between 10 p.m. and 2 a.m. 'I was a single mum,' she says, 'I had no choice. I got them to school, did the day job, then came home, I'd feed them, bathe them, then write my book.' But she tries to do less in the evenings now, and has adopted a relaxing night-time routine . . .

'I'm a huge believer in a bath. I have a shower to clean myself, a bath to relax. So I bathe in the evening – twice a week in the summer, maybe four times in winter, as it's lovely to be warm. I'm a big one for a long read in the bath, too – something that you'd never have time for. I like *Vanity Fair* for long reads. I love a New York society socialite scandal. A good 4000-worder. I also have an iPad in the corner of the bathroom and I'll listen to Desert Island Discs, or an audiobook.

'In terms of products, I use the cheap stuff in the shower and the expensive stuff in the bath. Lovely bubbles. In the shower, it's a waste, as it goes straight down the plughole. I like Laura Mercier Crème Brulee Honey Bath, Cowshed, Elemis Milk Bath. I like to make my selection according to mood: I choose a flavour according to how I feel. The Soap Co. are an amazing social enterprise entirely started by blind workers, and they make beautiful products. Clarins I like, too. Living Sea Therapy. In the shower I use Soaper Duper – it's cheaper and environmentally friendly. The kids like that, too.

'My products change all the time because of being sent samples through my work, but my routine is the same. At night-time I do a hot cloth cleanse, followed by some kind of serum, oil or night cream – sometimes both (in winter). And then in the morning, I use another hot cloth cleanse, a lighter milk and an acid. This is followed by a vitamin C serum and then a moisturiser. The players change a lot but the routine is always the same.

'Loads of times I've had too much wine and fallen asleep at my laptop, in my makeup. Or if I'm on a book deadline, I might let things slip. But I do try to keep on top of it – when you've had a baby, or you're in the middle of a work project, I do think that a skincare routine, showering, makeup – however you choose to do it – does provide a useful demarcation for the day. If you sit in pyjamas, the day can run away from you. Shower, clean your teeth, and you're ready to start working. If you dawdle, it's easy for your day to lose structure. For me, anyway.'

Quick tips for your night-time routine:

— **Have a bath with the kids:** it's a good way to get a relaxing soak in yourself before bed. If you can, hop in for a few minutes before adding the cold water and enjoy the hot water on your skin.

— **No screens for an hour before bed:** watching TV in the evenings is fine, as is doing your social media stuff, but log out with an hour before sleep time and read a book.

— Or, if you're not into novels, **how about using a relaxation app?** Headspace is great for mindfulness, Clementine has a dedicated 'sleep' section, the Calm app helps to reduce anxiety.

— **Make sure you're getting as close to eight hours as possible.** So count back from the time the baby/kids tend to wake up in the morning, and that's your bedtime.

— **Avoid caffeine in the late afternoon** and evening. Also sugary foods. I like to eat dinner early, with the kids, which ensures it's all digested before bed.

— **Start a skincare routine:** find products that smell and feel lovely on your skin. This will help you to relax before bed.

A monthly woman's issue

One monthly challenge that most women will face is menstruation. My periods took a while to return following childbirth and breastfeeding, which can stall the return (for this reason, I wanted to continue breastfeeding for ever). But when they did, they were horrific. Perhaps it was the loss of the oxytocin that flowed while I was breastfeeding and also my body readjusting as it returned to its fertile state, but whatever it was, I felt murderous for about a week in the lead-up to my period. I was spotty, angry, anxious, bloated and all the other shit that comes with the 'menses'. I'm not alone in finding this womanly issue fairly insurmountable at times.

Laura Alvarado, 30, lives with her son Jesse, aged five, and her boyfriend. She co-parents with Jesse's dad, and her boyfriend's son lives with them at weekends. Alongside parenting, Laura runs Tomato Tutors – a hugely successful holistic education studio and agency offering one-to-one and group classes for young people. I asked her how she manages co-parenting – with both her biological son, and her boyfriend's – alongside running a full-on business and doing freelance tutoring and Laura said that one important aspect of her monthly planning, in terms of work, is to pay close attention to her menstrual cycle. For instance, she arranges meetings with investors or other important engagements in the two weeks after she's had her period. This allows her to spend the two weeks prior looking after her body and mind; not putting too much pressure on herself, when she might be feeling more lethargic or out of sorts.

Anna Jones is similarly focused on fitting work around her menstrual cycle and with the help of Maisie Hill, the doula who helped deliver her son, charts her cycles. 'Being more aware has made me realise there are times in the month when I shouldn't be giving a talk to 500 people,' she says. 'Three days before period is not a good time for public speaking. Sometimes I have to do it but I'll notice that, while generally I don't feel nervous about public speaking, just before my period I do.' When she can, she uses the first week of her cycle for coming up with ideas and sending out emails. The second week, she'll cement what she came up with. In the third week, all being well, she'll tie up loose ends, then the week before her period she has a break.

'I'm at a point in my career now where I'm calling the shots so I have flexibility to do that,' she says. 'To even be able to send an email saying I've got really bad period pains – I couldn't do that for years, I felt like it was difficult to even say the word "period".' Anna explains that the 9–5, Monday–Friday working week was designed during the Industrial Revolution, built around men working – not women. This is why our very present, very affecting menstrual cycle isn't considered in the workplace. 'During the first week of my cycle, I could work 9 in the morning til 10 at night,' says Anna. 'Everything's firing. But day 26, I want to climb under a rock and start swearing. I feel excited for the generation of our children. It will take time to trickle through, but eventually girls will be taught there are different characteristics to a month.'

The idea of working around your menstrual cycle is becoming increasingly popular, as women pay more attention to their bodies and wellbeing. The Talented Ladies Club – an online resource for mothers who are passionate about their career or business – explains that you have four phases:

Menstruation phase: days 1–5
Follicular phase: days 1–13
Ovulation phase: day 14
Luteal phase: days 15–28.

This is approximate, cycles may differ by a few days, so the best way to work out your personal phases is to keep a diary for a few months. Note down when your period starts and ends and, if possible, when you ovulate. You can also keep a record of how you're feeling each day – energised, reflective, tired, creative, etc. – to track your mood patterns. So, which part of your menstrual cycle is best for what sort of work?

Menstruation – a great time for organisation, tidying and emotional and physical cleansing. So tackle tasks like restructuring your office or workspace, and eliminating unhelpful systems or baggage, filing and accounts.

Follicular – a creative, energetic time of the month for most women. It's also when our left brain is more dominant, making us better at verbal reasoning and learning. So it's a good time to embark on new projects and tackle trickier tasks that require dextrous thinking and enthusiasm.

Ovulation and luteal – a time when your thoughts are directed more inwardly. It's a reflective period in which we are better able to recognise and transform difficult areas of our lives and work. We're also more intuitive, making it a good time to make big decisions and plan strategies.[1]

4
The pram in the hall

'There are many women with children under five who want to work and who lack affordable, high-quality childcare.'

Harriet Harman

When planning how to balance children and work, the literary critic Cyril Connolly's famous quote springs to mind: 'There is no more sombre enemy of good art than the pram in the hall'. However, Cyril Connolly was not a freelance mum. He was a dad, who had children in his fifties. I've found, in fact, that having children has shaped my career: it has become the subject of much of my journalism, and is of course the basis for this book. However, attempting to have a full-time freelance career while looking after kids is unlikely to work. It's possible to dabble, and do part-time work – or even to rack up full-time hours when you're starting up. But I'm yet to meet a woman who manages to fully devote herself to both work and children, at the same time, permanently. It's too much. You may be happy to do smaller chunks of work and fit it around naps, evenings and weekend – and this is perfectly viable. But if you'd like to move on to the next stage, and devote more time to your freelance work, it's advisable to think about childcare.

Sarah Akwisombe, founder of No Bull Business School online social media courses, interior designer and mum of one, says: 'You just cannot work (properly) with kids around. Make sure you have a solid plan as to who will be looking after the kids, when, how much it's going to cost and a plan to escalate your childcare once you reach a certain income goal. Otherwise it's more difficult to grow and take on new clients.'

So, here are the childcare options – what you go for will be dependent on your working hours, your child's age and how much childcare you need. Every mum's situation is different. There is no right way to do this, just what's right for you and your family.

● ●

Nursery

Day nurseries take babies from as young as six weeks old, and up to the age of five. They are either private or run by the local authority, and often have extended opening hours – e.g. 7 a.m.–7 p.m. – to suit the 9–5 hours of working parents. The staff will be trained to create a stimulating, caring environment. My daughter went to a nursery from the age of 18 months, initially one day a week, then later two days. It took a month or so to settle, as there was a big gap between her nursery days each week, but she soon loved it. They provided all the food and entertainment,

8 a.m.–6 p.m., and I paid £50 a day. The average cost of full-time nursery for under twos in the UK is £232.84 per week.[1] After that, some two-year-olds will be eligible for 15 hours of free childcare, for example, if you get certain benefits.[2]

Advantages

— Extended hours; opening from as early as 7 a.m., closing at up to 8 p.m.

— It won't close down if a member of staff is ill.

— At some nurseries you can request extra hours if you have more work on.

— Your child will be out of your home, which is useful if that's where you're working.

— It's great for your child's 'social life', as there's the potential to make lots of new friends.

— They are generally open all-year-round, you won't have six-week summer holidays when you need to find a different childcare option.

Disadvantages

- There are more children in the space so it can feel like they will get a bit lost, though there are laws about staff–children ratios.

- Illness spreads very quickly around nurseries, so your child may pick up more bugs.

● ●

Preschool

Before children start in reception class they can attend a preschool, which is sometimes attached to a primary school. This is available from the age of three and at the moment, all children in England are entitled to 570 free hours of childcare per year – from an approved childcare provider (childminder or nursery). It's usually taken as 15 hours a week for 38 weeks of the year, but you can choose to take fewer hours over more weeks. My daughter turned three in June and in the September, we enrolled her for a preschool – a state-run nursery that is part of the school we'd like her to attend. Because my husband and I are both working, we qualified for 30 free hours of childcare a week – a government initiative to get mothers back into work. This made a huge difference to me, as I then only had one child to look after, Monday–Friday. Each parent needs to be earning at least the minimum wage for 16 hours of work a week, and less than £100,000.

Advantages

- It can potentially be attached to the school they will later attend, so it can help with settling them into their reception class.

- You might qualify for free childcare (some private nurseries and nannies don't offer this option).

Disadvantages

- Classes might be bigger than in a private nursery. Initially, my daughter's nursery felt very big and busy, but she quickly settled, we got to know the kids and staff and it now feels lovely and cosy.

- They close, like school, for all the holidays – half-term, two weeks at Easter, same for Christmas, six weeks in the summer.

Childminder

Childminders are Ofsted-registered and can look after your child from their home. They can care for up to six children at a time, including their own. No more than three of the children should be five or younger, and of these three only one can be under 12 months old in England, Scotland or Northern Ireland.[3] Childminders don't need formal childcare qualifications, but they are required to do a children's first aid course, and learn about kids' nutrition, food hygiene and health and safety. On average, you'll pay £107.41 per week for 25 hours of childcare.

Advantages

— If you like the idea of your child being around other children but in a more homely environment, this can work well.

— Your child will still qualify for the free childcare hours.

— There is often some flexibility in terms of hours, and some childminders will collect your child from your home.

— Usually, it will be one person providing all the childcare, unlike nurseries where there are lots of members of staff.

Disadvantages

— If the childminder is ill, childcare is cancelled.

• •

Shared workspace with crèche

Shared workspaces with an in-house crèche are becoming increasingly popular as more parents opt for the freelance career path. This is a very flexible way of working, as you can often sign up for your desk and childcare the day before, and you'll be close to your child while you work. It can also be more affordable, as you're only paying for the hours that you need childcare. However, some will also offer more formal arrangements, so that your child can attend a certain amount of days a week, like a stand-ard nursery. Prices will hugely vary depending on where you're based and what the space is like. But, as an example, Cuckooz Nest in London's Clerkenwell offers a fully flexible deal where there's no membership fee and you pay £23 per hour for workspace and crèche. There's a full list of UK shared workspaces with a crèche at the end of the book.

Advantages

— Allows for spontaneity, if a big job suddenly comes in.

— You'll be close to your baby or child.

— You don't have to financially commit to weekly or monthly payments.

Disadvantages

— Won't work so well if your child needs a nap.

— Staff may change so your child won't necessarily have a key worker or familiar person to hand them over to.

— As a long-term or permanent childcare option, it will be more expensive.

Nanny

A nanny will either be live-in or come to your house to look after your child(ren), and is an employee so will be entitled to sick pay, holiday pay, maternity/paternity leave, etc. They will be able to stick to the routine you have for your child, and offer one-on-one care. This means your child may be able to form more of an attachment to their nanny, and feel comforted by a closer relationship. The average take-home salary for a live-in nanny ranges from £302 to £351 per week, depending on where you live. Day nannies charge more, on average between £405 and £476.[4] They don't need any formal qualifications.

Advantages

- They fit in with you and your family, rather than the other way round.

- Your child may settle more easily with a childcare arrangement in their own home.

Disadvantages

— It is a more expensive option, though 'nanny shares' – where you team up with another family – can work well.

— There will be periods where she is entitled to holiday and you won't have any childcare.

— Likewise, if she's ill the childcare won't be available.

— It's in your home, so you might have to work elsewhere if you find your children distracting.

• •

Au pair

This will usually be a young person from outside of the UK who comes to live with you and your family. They are paid a small amount to look after your children, when you need it, in exchange for a room and food. Often, they'll be keen to learn English and this will be their motivation for coming to stay in the UK. They might be able to babysit in the evenings and do light housework. Usually, if an au pair works 25 hours a week, you'll pay £70. For 30 hours a week, it should be at least £85. Additional babysitting requires extra payment.

Advantages

— They will be living with you which might offer more flexibility for ad-hoc work, if a job comes in.

— Your children will get to know them very well.

— It can be nice to introduce someone from a different country and culture to your children.

Disadvantages

— They don't need any formal qualifications and may have never looked after children before, so if you have very young children, this might not work so well.

— It can be difficult sharing your home with another adult, especially when your children are young and perhaps waking in the night.

Babysitters (apps, websites)

If you need irregular childcare, babysitters can work well. Perhaps a local parent friend can recommend one. Or you could try using an app like Bubble – you put in the date and times and every available babysitter in your area pops up with a profile and their hourly rate. The app connects to social media so if you have mutual friends on Facebook, for example, this will be highlighted. Also the websites childcare.co.uk and sitters.co.uk offer options for finding a local babysitter. You'll pay from £6–£12 per hour, depending on location and their experience.

Advantages

— This can be arranged last-minute.

— You only pay for the hours you need.

Disadvantages

— You probably won't have met this person before and won't have the opportunity to interview them prior to their arrival (except on the phone).

Childcare swap

If you have a friend who is also freelance, you could do a childcare swap: you take her child two days a week, she takes yours for two days. Or you have both kids on weekday mornings, while she does afternoons. That way, there is no extra cost to either of you. It works nicely if you meet for lunch and all catch up before handing the kids over to the other mum for the second half of the day.

Taking your child to work

When Alex Hoffler, co-founder of The Meringue Girls bakery, had a baby, she wanted to continue working but also to be with her daughter, Indi. After three months' maternity leave, she started taking Indi into the Meringue Girls bakery off Broadway Market in Hackney, and along to meetings. As a newborn baby, this was fine – she mostly slept and fed. But as she got older, it became more difficult. 'We had to take her to Dubai on what turned out to be a pretty disastrous work trip to look at franchising the business,' she says. 'She was five months, and puked and pooed everywhere on both flights. It was such a surreal experience, carting her around shopping malls looking at potential bakery sites, trying to be professional and get my head around being a new mum and the breastfeeding – in a very male-dominated, foreign environment.'

Eventually, Alex found it too stressful and so arranged a more formal childcare arrangement: 'I was constantly asking friends and co-workers to take her around the block so we could have a meeting or do an important call. It wasn't really fair on them, so at six months, we managed to find a nanny share situation with another local baby for a couple of days a week, and I've slowly clawed my way back to five days a week, but still only 9.30 a.m.–3 p.m. Indi's now three and a half. I can't get my head around how I'm going to do it again with another baby in May, but you just make it work when you're in it.'

Carrie Anne Roberts has worked around her son River since his birth. She tried a nursery but he didn't settle and she didn't feel comfortable about leaving him, so instead he'd join her on photoshoots or watch a film while she made and packed orders in their home. If you want to do it, it's possible to take your baby/child to work. Greg Stanton (@london_dad) wrote a post about taking his children to meetings with him. He tells companies who don't like this that if his children aren't welcome, he can't work with them. This requires you to be fairly brazen, though: either just turning up with the baby or telling clients that you'll be bringing your children to meetings.

However, we have the power to change the culture. When my son was tiny and I was asked to attend a government focus group on flexible working, I said I'd be bringing my exclusively breastfed, three-month-old baby along. The event organiser said I couldn't. There was lots of emailing and many phone conversations until I said: If he's not welcome, I'm not coming. It seemed ludicrous to be discussing flexible work and to turn away a mother who couldn't leave her baby at home. Eventually, someone high up contacted me, apologising and saying he was welcome, but for me it was too late – I felt excluded, and like I was a nuisance. I didn't go, but I did write an article about it, explaining the importance of making mothers feel included. Sometimes this will mean bringing a baby, and if the mother's cool with this, everyone else should be, too. I'm always open to people bringing their children along to work meetings. Sometimes it's distracting but people only do it if there's no other option. If we can all keep an open mind about this, the culture will start to change.

• •

Get your partner to do their bit

If you live with your children's father, or are co-parenting, make sure he's as involved as possible. Sadly, only 2 per cent of dads take the shared parental leave they are entitled to. A big culture shift is required before more men will be offered this leave, or ask for it and are willing to take longer than the standard two weeks' paternity leave. They need to be told and to feel that they are as vital to their children's lives as the mothers. Unbelievably, a freelance dad isn't entitled to shared parental leave at all, but at the time of writing there's a petition being circulated that is asking the government to introduce new laws that will change this. Watch this space.

However, sharing the responsibility for childcare is also a personal choice. I wanted to have the first year with my babies so my husband and I agreed that's what we'd do. I was breastfeeding and needed to recover from two (physically) traumatic births. But once my body was working again, and breastfeeding was easing off, he started to take on more of the childcare. This allowed me to go and do talks in the daytime, or to agree to last-minute commissions (the online journalism culture is: Annie, can you write an 800-word article in two hours? So a partner with flexible work is very helpful. As are grandparents you can ask for help. Or a local friend or neighbour). You need to make it work for you and your family, but just don't feel your freelance career has to come second. You matter, and so does your work.

One issue that may arise is the fact that at least one of you needs to be earning money to support the family. When you're starting up, you might not be raking it in, but the idea is that at some point, you will be. So if your partner is able to help out a bit more in the initial stages – definitely when he's not at work, in the evenings or weekends, but also by taking the odd day off to help you when you're starting up – this can be seen as an investment in the future. Once your freelance career is up and running, you will be bringing in an income. But to make this happen you'll need your partner's belief and support. Have this conversation. Treat it as payment in lieu: work now, get paid later. And it goes without saying that the cleaning, cooking and other domestic duties should be divided fifty-fifty.

This was important for Holly Tucker, she says: 'I was lucky enough that my husband, Frank, decided to give up his career to be a full-time dad to Harry. He really is the most incredible role model to him, and it makes my heart so full to see the amazing bond they have. Frank is still the wind beneath my wings, and both he and Harry are a constant support to me with everything I do at Holly & Co. In fact, Harry has now become our official apprentice at the shop, and loves nothing more than coming to work. He's even set up his own small business called The Sugar Boy (@sugarboy.co), selling sweets packed with emotions, to help kids deal with how they're feeling. I don't know where he gets it from!'

Anna Jones discussed childcare with her husband as soon as she became pregnant, and they agreed that it would be split down the middle. Both working for themselves meant there was scope for flexibility, so if Anna has a busy period, he can pick up the slack in terms of childcare, and the same in reverse. 'Both of us have designed our lives to be flexible – it's not something that has happened by chance,' says Anna. 'It's been a longer-term plan.' However, she has encountered the same difficulties that many mothers do: the mum takes maternity leave, and then suddenly, even if the actual childcare doesn't fall to her, the *arranging* of it does. It adds to her mental load. But when the nursery began to automatically call her if there was a problem – 'in society, it's assumed that the mother will be primary caregiver' – she wrote a polite email asking for them to contact her husband, too, and that was the end of that.

Bertie Bowen, stylist and one-half of @mothershoppers, recommends syncing your calendar with your partner. 'I'm not a naturally organised person,' she says, 'so being a mother to two and married to another creative freelancer is sometimes chaotic. We synced our calendars on our phones so we can easily look at what we are doing each day. We both put in the days we are working, then extras such as events for me or band practice for him, as well as social commitments. Plus the days the kids are at nursery. It has saved a lot of arguments!'

What to do if the kids are ill

On the subject of partners doing their bit, if your child is ill this can create something of a dilemma in terms of childcare. Sickness means time away from your childcare provider, so one of you will have to forgo work and look after the kids. The way we do it is this: if my daughter is ill and I'm already looking after my son (for instance, it's not one of the two days he's at nursery), I'll also look after her. But if he's at nursery and I have important work to do, my husband will take time off work. If I can manage my workload in the evening or at nap-time, I'll do it. We work it out between us, but it's not simply assumed that because I work from home, I'll do it. Make it a conversation, not an assumption.

School's out for summer

Until last year, my daughter was at a private nursery, which meant it ran all year round, closing only for two weeks in August and two weeks in December. So I had two days a week of guaranteed childcare all but four weeks of the year. But then she started preschool and was only in childcare during term time. Suddenly, I had her with me for two weeks at Easter, every half term and SIX WEEKS over the summer. My son's childminder also worked only in the term time, which left me with no childcare for a fair few months across the year. I know parents who use summer schools, send their kids to acting classes or sports weeks over the holidays or do swaps with other parents. How I've made it work is to look at my schedule week by week. If I don't have much on, I look after them both full-time and work when my son naps (and daughter watches TV), or in the evenings. But other weeks, when I have meetings or work commitments, I've used the Bubble babysitting app for ad-hoc childcare. The hourly rate is more expensive – £12 rather than the £5 an hour for nursery – but I could book her to come for just a few hours, to cover the time I was working. And it meant I wasn't paying someone to be there when my son was sleeping. If you know you're working a day a week, or two, or five, it's worth planning childcare in advance to cover the nursery/school/childminder holidays.

Check if you're eligible for financial help

As mentioned earlier, all children in England are entitled to 570 free hours of childcare per year – from an approved childcare provider (childminder or nursery) – from the age of three. And you may be able to claim Tax-Free Childcare – up to £500 every three months (£2000 a year) for each of your children to help with the costs of childcare. There is additional help available for parents who have a disability, or have children with special needs.

How other freelancing mums make it work:

Journalist Robyn Wilder has two boys, aged three and six months: 'I have my kids with a part-time nanny four mornings a week. It sort of works. I can take them to the playground in the afternoons and pitch and invoice from my phone in the evenings in front of the TV.'

Photographer Penny Wincer has two school-aged children: 'Neither of my kids attended a nursery till they were preschool age. The hours are just too restrictive, plus I couldn't ever cancel a shoot just because my child threw up the night before and wasn't allowed to attend. Nannies are a lot more affordable than people assume, especially once you have two or more kids. My two were looked after ad-hoc by a nanny on a casual week-by-week arrangement until my youngest was three. I was ready to increase my work load then (with school and preschool hours contributing to my childcare) so that was the point at which I employed a nanny on a permanent basis, on a salary, three days a week. There are lots of different ways of approaching childcare, so don't assume that you won't find someone great who can be flexible with you and affordable. I have a couple of babysitters who are my backup for when the nanny takes holidays or is unwell and I can't avoid shooting.'

Pragya Agarwal says: 'It is important that we do not feel guilty about sending children to nursery or daycare when needed. My two-year-old twins are now going to a lovely Montessori nursery three days a week and these days are so important for me to get some mental and physical space to focus on my work.

This is crucial for me to stay sane, so that when I am with them I am content and happy, and so are they. Since I am working for myself, I can be flexible. There are days when I can only find time to work after 9 p.m. and work until 2 or 3 a.m., and there are days when I can only fit this in during their afternoon naps. But it has also taught me to be highly efficient and productive, as I know how valuable my time is.'

Anna Jones was offered a *Guardian* column when her son was three months old. 'Not dream timing, but I couldn't turn it down,' she says. So she said yes, then relied on her mum coming two days a week to help out while she wrote. Her husband also helped out more. And in terms of food styling – done outside of the home – she'd bring the baby along, so that she could breastfeed him. Now he's two, and goes to nursery two days a week – short days – has a day with a childminder and a day with Anna's mum. 'I try to cram everything in so I can be around as much as I can be,' she says. And she'll pick him up early from childcare when the workload is lighter.

Cherry Healey has two children, aged eight and four. She has separated from her children's father, but they co-parent and Cherry has an au pair living with her.

'I'm a single mum,' she says, 'but there are lots of different degrees of co-parenting. My mum is nearby. I have a lot of support. I see that the golden nugget is the extra bedroom we have – my kids share their room and our au pair lives in the third bedroom. But that's such a privileged position to be in; most people live in a two-bed place, if they have kids. She's really important for us. My schedule changes all the time so the deal is she never has to work weekends – my ex, or boyfriend, or mum are around. And often, I don't work weekends. So she gets time off, but she has to be flexible. Sometimes she does the school run. I love doing it, and so does my ex, but sometimes she has to do it – and has to change her plans at the last minute. It means if I leave at 5 a.m., for filming, the kids don't have to get up. They can stay at home, in their pyjamas and have their breakfast. The au pair allows me to come back at midnight if we've been filming and everything's shifted because someone's turned up late. It's really difficult with documentaries to guarantee everything running on time. It's hard sharing our home but that's the payoff. Also, I'm like a surrogate mum to her, which is sometimes emotionally hard when I'm tired, but I see the flexibility that she gives me.'

Lucy Mangan was freelance before giving birth to her son. 'I'd envisaged getting back to work as quickly as possible,' she says. But a difficult birth and long recovery period made this difficult. 'I was unable to sit or stand properly,' she says. She spent the first few months living with her mum, who could help with her son, so that when he was six months old, she was back to working more regularly. 'I don't really remember how I worked,' she says. 'But having postnatal depression meant I wasn't interested in my baby so I felt no real longing to get back to him. If you're depressed, it's quite easy to work, as you don't feel that tension about leaving them. But also, I'm the main breadwinner so I had no choice: I had to work.' When her son turned three, he started nursery. 'Any set freedom is a godsend,' she says. 'You learn to pack it all in and crack on. Interestingly, having less time to work makes little difference to the quality of your work.'

Amy Rose, writer and editor, has one three-year-old son: 'When I first launched The Fourth Trimester online magazine and became freelance, I would take Milo to his grandparents' house and work from there, then they could look after him but if he needed a feed I was there. When he turned one we put him into nursery for a couple of mornings a week and that helped massively – I would get as much work done as possible during those hours and then carry on when he got home and napped. If I had too much work then I would work in the evenings and sometimes early morning – nursery was expensive so it was important that I didn't say no to any work! Nowadays he is at nursery Monday to Thursday 8 a.m.–1.30 p.m. and I work during that time and sometimes pay for extra sessions if I have a meeting or event to go to, but as he is three we get 30 hours' free childcare. In September he will be going to school so I will be taking on more clients (hopefully!).'

Eirlie Chisholm is raising her two young boys alone. They go to nursery two days a week: 'The fact that there is no other income in the house to rely on is a huge pressure, it means I need to find time to have another job that pays for childcare, food, transport, clothes, etc. If I'm sick, there is no choice but to keep going, no one can tell me to take it easy while they take care of the kids so I can rest. I think that's the hardest part, being unwell and still needing to be carer, cleaner, chef, provider, etc. And if my children are sick and can't go to nursery then those days are a write-off too – it can mean a whole week goes by without childcare, which I find very stressful. When you rely so heavily on a couple of days of childcare to align perfectly with your job, it's really hard to cope when things don't go right. You have to leave the job to get your child. Or feel like a terrible mother for begging the staff to let him stay a bit longer so you can get your work done. I work if my children nap. I work most evenings from when they go to bed until I can't keep my eyes open any longer. I work about three–four hours in the evening and it's quite easy to be focused on work at night when you're a solo parent, as there is no partner around that needs your attention, which I quite like for the most part! My biggest treat to myself is going to bed early, and having long baths during a nursery day. I have to stop myself from working every night, because I find that I often feel burnt out by the time I get to nursery days, and then I'm terribly unproductive.'

Zoë de Pass has a son at school, a daughter at nursery and a third baby on the way: 'Juggling childcare is really hard when you are freelance because you can't commit to a set amount of days – you have to take the leap and either commit to the childcare or work and then make it fit.' She took the leap and committed to part-time childcare so that she could grow her brand, and is now able to work from home, collaborating with brands on new clothes and shoe designs and promoting products.

Author and lecturer Anna Whitwham has one four-year-old daughter: 'My situation changed a lot because my mum got very ill and had lots of cancer treatment. She has always been my main source of childcare. I put Sylvie into nursery two days a week to cover my lecturing days, and did all my book writing at night, 8–11, and edits in coffee shops when I could find a golden hour. All very tiring, but I tried to see this as a phase and not permanent, it's do-able. And it's life – everyone has to get tired. There is an end point. I also made a decision not to try to write in the daytime when I wasn't working and had Sylvie. This was mainly to do with having a clear head for writing fiction, but also about enjoying the time with her fully. It was so good for our souls. So, I suppose my life is blocked out a lot more now. And I know when I can work, and when I can't, and that way I panic a little less about the passing of time and I value the hour or two alone in a coffee shop doing edits, or planning a seminar.'

When Sali Hughes' second son, Arthur, was two and a half, she hired an au pair. She found it difficult having someone living with them, as it meant she had no privacy, but she says, 'With my job, I couldn't have daycare or nursery because I don't work normal hours. I might be hosting an event on Wednesday night, then at a literary festival on Saturday but around all through the week. It is simply the only form of childcare that you can have as someone who works unconventional hours. There was nothing wrong with my au pairs, they were good to the kids. And I couldn't have done without. But it has its challenges.' Now that her sons are older – 13 and 11 – they're able to look after themselves a bit more. 'We live next door to school, and the kids let themselves in. Though there's pretty much always someone here now.' (Sali is now married to a comedy writer and he works from home, mostly.) But occasionally, they'll both be working over a weekend and her sons will either stay with their dad, go with Sali to a literary festival or overnight stay while she works, or she'll ask a friend to have them for a sleepover. 'You patch something together,' she says.

5
Fake it till you make it

'I used to walk down the street like I was a superstar . . . I want people to walk around delusional about how great they can be – and then to fight so hard for it every day that the lie becomes the truth.'

Lady Gaga

Becoming a mother is transformative: you have a new responsibility and focus in life, alongside everything that was important to you before: work, relationship, family, friends, hobbies. This can feel amazing and fulfilling, but it can also cause you to question your place in the world and your identity. Who am I, now that I've had children? Am I still important in the workplace? Does my partner find me attractive as a mother? Do my friends think I'm boring? What clothes should I wear, as a mum? (Answer: whatever the hell you want.)

While you're transitioning from woman to mother – through pregnancy, birth and the early days with a newborn – your confidence can take a knock. Your body's changing, your relationship with the people around you – at work and at home – may alter, your thoughts about what's important might shift and evolve. However, you're just as valuable in terms of your career, as a worker, than you were before you had children. Becoming a mother doesn't make you useless, or less intelligent. On the contrary, it can teach you valuable new skills: negotiation, patience, prioritising, delegating, responsibility, team work, putting someone else first. But it might take you some time to realise, or feel, this.

Anna Jones shared her thoughts with me on the transition into motherhood: 'I found the first six months the hardest. My son was a really needy baby and just cried constantly. Some babies are chilled, some aren't. I spent months just jiggling him – then passing him to my mum or husband to jiggle. So the motherhood transition was a bit of a shock. I had a difficult birth – not the pool at home I'd imagined; I ended up with an emergency C-section and a brutal, savage recovery. You have a vision of what motherhood will be like, but my birth was the perfect example of how you can't control everything. You have to accept and compromise. I did find the birth amazing, although it was a C-section – it was a conscious, amazing birth. But then three months in, I was offered a *Guardian* column and ended up stepping back into the world of work, which felt really soon. My brain and hormones hadn't returned to normal. I usually have a strong sense of right and wrong – and I did with my son – but with the rest of my life, I couldn't access the decision-making process.'

Anna managed to keep the *Guardian* column going, write a cookbook and continue with her career, although she wishes someone had been honest about how hard it would be. 'There's another female chef who, when I was pregnant, said: "Babies just sleep all the time. You'll be able to write the book." I'd signed a contract when I was pregnant – and I had a year and a half to do it. So I thought, fantastic, I'll just pop him on the floor and knock a book out. But it's not like that. Writing cookery books is an interactive process – you have to cook the food before writing it down. Details need to be checked.' However, she did manage to write it, and it was published. Now that her son is older, and more self-sufficient, Anna says that the challenges are changing. 'Now, the hardest thing is that I really miss him when he's at nursery. I want to be a present mother, though, and I am. I collect him early when work is lighter, rather than doing housework or driving new projects.'

• •

Be a swan

What it took for me to pick up on one of my skills, as a mother, was a generous comment from a neighbour. I was getting the kids out of the door one morning. My son was about six weeks old and my daughter was two and a half. We were going to a storytelling class. My neighbour watched me push the buggy out and said: 'You're always so calm and together.' She said that she never felt like that, with her kids. What she didn't know (until I told her) was that my anxiety had rocketed, and that very morning I'd rushed around and panicked and fretted while trying to get everyone ready on time. I didn't feel in the least bit calm. I'd probably also shed some tears.

After I'd told her this, she said: 'You're like a swan then. Graceful above water but paddling frantically underneath.' And while I hesitate to compare myself to a swan, as it feels rather grandiose, I like that analogy. It was exactly how I felt: I can rush and feel crazed indoors but when I present myself to the outside world, I will appear as if I have it all under control. That was my way of coping. It helped me to get through the rest of the day, knowing that it was possible to look – and even feel – calm, once the initial morning chaos had passed. This is now a skill I recognise in myself: being able to maintain a calm exterior, even if I feel anxious inside. It's useful when meeting with difficult clients, as well as when dealing with my children.

Lean in

In business, there is definitely something to be said for appearing confident, even if you don't feel it. Women often hold back when it comes to new work opportunities, or asking for a higher day rate. In Sheryl Sandberg's *Lean In*, she discusses the different ways a man and woman look at a job spec. A man will pick out all the qualities or experience that he does have, and apply. While a woman will see everything that she can't do, or hasn't done before, and won't apply. This is the reason why women hold just 12 per cent of full-time jobs paying £150,000 or more.[1] So even if you're feeling low in confidence, you should still put yourself forward. Because the likelihood is that you CAN do it, if you want to.

Confidence-building

I attended a confidence workshop with life coach Pattie Horrocks. She explained that confidence is about believing in yourself. Accepting yourself. Embracing your imperfections and being able to say:

I gave it a shot, I did my best. On that day, at that time, I did the best job possible. And then move on, don't dwell. She said that we need to be kind to ourselves, because some days we won't perform well. But that doesn't matter. Pattie emphasised the importance of practising gratitude; of focusing on the good things in your life. The small achievements, as well as the big ones (sometimes that might be just getting through the day). I asked Pattie if she believed in 'fake it till you make it'. And she said yes, if you believe you can do it, you'll find a way.

She then talked us through a visualisation for confidence-building:

— Imagine a circle on the floor in front of you – your 'circle of excellence'.

— Relax, breathe, centre yourself.

— Then think of a positive experience, when you've felt confident – what can you see/hear/smell/taste/feel? Really take yourself back into that experience.

— Mentally project those feelings into the circle in front of you.

- When it feels strong, step into the circle, turn up the volume of your sensations, get the strength of the experience and feel it in your body.

- Then create a gesture to anchor that feeling. Maybe you could clap your hands, or squeeze your thumb and forefinger together.

- Step out of the circle and disassociate from the experience. Shake off your hands and feet.

The idea is that when you are next in a difficult situation, or feeling unconfident, you can use that anchor (e.g. clapping your hands) and it will take you back to how you felt in your circle of excellence: calm, centred, in control. Pattie also shared tips for preparing yourself for an important work meeting, or public speaking, or meeting a new client – all situations that might make you feel nervous. Here are Pattie's tips:

- Plan, prepare, do your homework. Find out as much as you can about the situation and people concerned in advance.

- Be clear about what you want from the situation.

- Rehearse what you want to say with a friend or colleague.

- Know your strengths and areas for development.

- List your strengths and celebrate them, feel good about them.

- Be aware of areas where you're not so strong and find ways to address them.

- Accept compliments and compliment yourself.

- Enjoy your own successes!

- Use negative feedback as a learning experience: how can you do things differently next time?

- Stay positive and offer others compliments.

Believe in yourself

Suzy Ashworth agrees about the power of confidence. 'Have you ever noticed how nine times out of ten, it's the person who everyone thinks is going to get the promotion who gets the promotion?' she says. 'Why is that? Because they've already been doing the job, or acting like they've been doing the job, for months in advance – making their interview a foregone conclusion. Decide where you want to go and start acting like you're already there and watch the magic happen.' This is what I did with getting a book deal. I told people that I was going to be writing a book before I actually had the deal. In time, it really did happen.

Sometimes a lack of confidence stems from fear: what if I go freelance and don't get any clients? What if I ask for a higher day rate and they say no? Will my friends think I'm failing if I only have 100 followers on Instagram? Suzy recommends embracing your fears. 'Do the thing that you know you should be doing, or really want to but that scares the bejesus out of you. That's the thing you know you should do! As with every scary thing you've ever done, it's never as scary as you think it's going to be and the first time is always the worst. Once you've got through the first time: reflect, learn, rinse and repeat.' So if you've set your mind on earning £500 a day from your work, make that your rate. If you want to do a TEDx talk, speak about it as if it's going to happen and then make it your mission.

Initially, you won't know everything about freelancing. You might know very little. But no one else needs to know that. If you make out that you're already successful, you soon will be (trust me, this is exactly what I did. At first I felt like a fraud but in time, when I really was earning good money and getting the commissions, I started to own it and feel proud). Part of this comes from recognising your strengths, and asking for what you deserve. There's always a temptation to work for free, at the start, for 'portfolio work', but this just puts you in the minds of those clients – or editors in my case – as someone who will work hard and doesn't need payment. If it will help with your PR to do a guest blog post (I've done lots), or to trial a new product by giving it out for free, do. If not, set a price, ask for it, do the work, get paid.

• •

Blow your own trumpet

And when you've done the job really well and have the money in your bank? Shout about it. 'Everyone loves a safe and confident pair of hands,' says Suzy. 'I mean, no one wants to be operated on by a surgeon who apologises every ten words and says it was everyone on the team but her who did anything, do they? When you rock it – own it! Tell your peers, your clients, your Facebook friends . . . let them know what you have achieved.' And the more people see you succeeding with your work, the more likely they will be to come to you when they need a freelancer in your field of expertise.

. . . .

Keep your 'success' stories to hand

I have a folder in my email account called 'special' and it's where I keep any lovely, encouraging, supportive emails. So if someone says I've done a really good job, or thanks me for something I've written that's helped them in some way, I file the email away in the 'special' folder. I also have a rejection folder that I've renamed 'got to keep', because I like the idea that one day I'll look back at all the rejections I've received and be able to laugh about it. But I spend more time looking at the 'special' folder, as it gives me a boost. Freelance social media specialist Nicola Washington (@ toomuchmotheringinformation) also recommends keeping a note of positive feedback. 'Write it down somewhere, keep a record on your phone. Every time you add something you'll see all the other positive feedback there and it will help to combat the funk of being freelance and having no one except you (and your bank account) take an interest in your professional development or successes.'

6
How to stand out on social media

It's estimated that there are 1.968 billion active mobile social-media users.[1]

Alongside your website, you'll need to have a presence on social media. It's expected of every freelancer and business these days. Put bluntly: if you don't, it's like you don't exist (sad, but true). There are so many social media platforms out there and some will be better suited to your work than others. For instance, if you're doing visual work, illustration or graphic design, Instagram is probably the one for you. If you're a writer, Twitter can be good. Most authors have a Twitter account. If your work is in PR or marketing, Facebook can be great for setting up groups for people doing similar work.

According to Business Insider,[2] the most-used social media platforms in 2017 were – in this order – Facebook, Instagram, Twitter. I'm on all three platforms, though some work better for me than others. This is largely down to how much time I invest in each, and the ones I like best. I find the community of mums on Instagram really supportive and I never get troll-y messages. Facebook is great for posts that I want people to share, as it's so easy to do this there (not so easy on Instagram). Twitter, I use for picking up PR requests and connecting with editors and journalists. There is something to be said, however, for having fewer platforms – even focusing just on one, initially

– and doing it really well. You don't want to spread yourself too thin, and each platform will require some commitment. Also, once you have followers on Instagram, for example, you can launch a Facebook page and ask them to join you over there, too.

Once you've decided which channel you're launching on, you'll need to decide on your handle (this is what people type in to find you; your social media name – on most channels this is preceded by '@'). Ideally, you'll have either your own name or the name of your website as your handle. On Instagram and Twitter, I'm @annieridout. This makes it easy for people to find me. If your name is already taken, you can add underscores or dots, but be sparing. And don't start with an underscore, as it means when people start typing your name, e.g. 'A' for Annie Ridout, it won't pop up in the search if your handle starts with this: _.

Like everyone, you'll start with no followers. How you build a following will depend on how much time and energy you put into it. Don't even think about buying followers, or 'follow for a follow' or following loads of people so that some follow you back and then you unfollow them. It might work initially, but it's not sustainable. I know, because I tried it. I wouldn't stoop to buying followers but I tried to trick the

Instagram algorithm by following maybe 100 people a day and seeing what happened. About 60 would follow me back. Then I could unfollow those 100 and my followers would grow without the amount of people I was following changing. However, it's a lazy and flawed plan. Those followers won't engage with your content in the same way as someone who's come to you because they like your brand, or have been tagged in a post, or relate to you and what you're about. And eventually they'll unfollow.

However, do be generous with follows. If you like an account or find someone who's doing work in your industry and you might be able to learn something from them, or collaborate in some way, follow them. There is a largely unspoken notion that being followed by thousands of people while only following a few hundred yourself is the desired position to be in, and that it somehow makes you 'cool'. But this is outdated. Now, it's cool to be kind. Frankie Tortora, who runs the excellent freelance parent website and Facebook group Doing It For The Kids, told me that any time a freelance parent follows her, she follows back. It's about being inclusive, welcoming and giving as well as taking. It's not about #followforafollow, it's just about being generally supportive.

But ultimately, like everything in business, if you want to grow a big, loyal following, the more time you devote to it, the sooner it will happen. Engaging with other people on Instagram will gain you followers: look at people's posts, comment, have conversations. Make yourself visible. And send people from one social account to another – write a tweet about something you've posted on Instagram. Tell your Facebook friends that you've started a (brilliant) Instagram account and ask them to come and follow you. It doesn't matter if you grow your following slowly, it matters that they care about your brand and will be loyal. My followers respond when I post. They ask questions. They tag their friends in the comments. They are loyal to me and I'm loyal to them – I've developed lots of relationships that have been brought into the real world. If I'm looking for support with an idea, the wonderful Instagram community of mums will often jump up to help.

Kids and online privacy

If you're launching a parenting brand, you'll need to decide what your views are on incorporating your kids in your online profile. When I launched The Early Hour, I used to post about my daughter, put up photos and use her name. As my following grew, I became concerned about her safety and privacy. The idea of someone seeing her in the street and knowing her name and various facts about her life didn't sit comfortably – also, my husband's not on social media and didn't want our kids to be. So I stopped posting front-on photos of their faces, only photographing from the back or side, or if their heads were cropped out or distorted. I also stopped using their names, referring to them instead as my 'son' and 'daughter' or 'the baby' and 'the preschooler'. At this point, my following stopped growing quite as quickly. My most popular posts had always been the ones about my family and home life – people like to be nosy (I certainly do) and know about all the behind-closed-doors stuff. But I decided to forgo followers in order to respect my family's privacy. Each parent will need to make their own decision on this, including you.

I will, however, reveal details about myself. After giving birth to my son, I shared a post about how battered and emotional I felt. Breastfeeding was excruciatingly painful, my nipples were bleeding, I was exhausted and my boobs were about to burst as my milk had just come in. It was a raw, personal post and I put it out spontaneously; this was my experience of new motherhood, and I wanted to be honest, rather than pretend it was all cosy cuddles with a newborn. People responded well, as this was relatable. It made them feel closer to me and my experience. Again, you can decide how much you reveal about yourself. Do what feels comfortable. I couldn't think of how this might backfire for me, as my feeling is that if I put it out there, I might make another mother's journey less lonely or overwhelming. I'm always reassured by other mums talking about the challenges, as well as the good stuff.

Anna Jones is @we_are_food, and has 147,000+ followers. She gives her thoughts on online sharing: 'Instagram is harder since having a kid. Before I can set up a shot, coffee will be spilled, or food swiped off the table. And I'm still trying to work out what level of sharing I'm comfortable with. Sometimes I feel like an imposter, because I connect with people who are sharing what's going on for them – and I find that very powerful. But I find when I share personal or political stuff, I get people dropping off, or sending private messages. I'm still going to talk about issues that I really care about, but in general, I'm not just constantly sharing. It's a vulnerability thing. We all feel a commitment to share in a consistent way but actually, sometimes it's better to not put anything up for a week. My husband isn't on social media so he isn't comfortable with me sharing family photos.'

Research, engage, innovate

To gain followers, you'll need to devote time to engaging with people on Instagram, and generally being active on social media, but also, do research about what works for other Instagrammers in your field, borrow ideas, look at the trends and then come up with your own original, innovative ideas. Molly Gunn has over 115k followers, and she keeps them coming by doing brilliant things like the InstaZine she launched in March 2018. She had seen how much time mums spend on Instagram and the only way of linking to content being through your Instagram profile, rather than in posts. This means people are more inclined to stay within the app then veer out to read articles or blogs. So she brought the content into Instagram. The idea is that each week, nine photos are posted on the @selfishmother Instagram feed, containing magazine-style content: beauty products, snappy articles – spread across multiple images, so you swipe through the carousel for the next part of the article – and fashion shoots. Such a clever way to use an existing platform.

Get shout-outs on social media

The best way to get new followers on any social media platform is to secure a shout-out or endorsement from someone in your field who has loads of followers. My followers shot up by 300 in a matter of minutes following a mention from an influential mum with lots of followers. But you'll need to be cunning about this. In the early days of my Instagram account, I posted a photo of myself in a 'Mother' jumper by Selfish Mother. They repost images of women in their clothes on their feed, so when they didn't repost mine, I wondered if they hadn't seen it. I messaged Molly and asked what had happened. She very politely explained that they only repost a few – not every selfie some random mum takes. I felt like an idiot. I still do. The best way to get people tagging you on social media or talking about your work, is by getting to know these people, or interviewing them for your blog then asking if they'd mind mentioning the article. Usually people are quite generous in this respect, but some people aren't. Try not to be annoyed if they don't link through or mention you or the article; they've got their own feeds and followers to think about.

Top tips for growing a big, loyal following on social media:

●●●●●●●●●●●●●●●●●●●●●●●●●●●

Facebook

— **On Facebook, you can create a 'page'**
for your freelance work, or business. Here you can post links to your blog or website, pictures of new products or write about what's going on, business-wise. To gain followers for your page, invite your existing Facebook friends, ask people from Instagram and Twitter to follow you over there, add a direct link to it from your website.

— **Sarah Turner (The Unmumsy Mum),** says: 'I hate overuse of the word "organic" but my Facebook page really did grow on its own without me having set my sights on a large following at the beginning. I think I owe its success to a number of things, including the timing of when I set the page up (2014, when there weren't quite so many parenting pages doing the Facebook rounds), several of my blog posts going viral quite early on and the fact that it has become almost like an online parenting community – posts from other mums and dads on my page are often just as successful, if not more successful, than the stuff I write!'

— Another idea is to **start a group dedicated to your field.** For instance, if you're a yoga teacher, start a group about yoga. People can post their own ideas, videos and challenges, and other likeminded people can respond. Groups are about giving, offering a platform for people to connect. But of course, you'll gain respect and will be subtly growing your following, as you're the leader.

- **Frankie Tortora started Doing It For The Kids,** a private Facebook group for freelancing parents that quickly had over 1000 members. I'm part of it and it's great. Parents ask about accounting, balancing work and home life as a freelancer, freelance lunch ideas. She says: 'A Facebook group is perfect for building a community of people who are all in the same situation. There's no hierarchy – everybody's just on the same level, talking to one another as fellow freelancing parents no matter who they are, what their social media "currency" is, or what they do for a living.'

- In terms of **what's expected of you, as admin for the group** Frankie says: 'Running the group was pretty exhausting for the first three to six months, I had to come up with a schedule for the week, ideas for regular threads, rules and so on. And the way to really get a group off the ground is to lead by example so I was just relentlessly posting questions, or links to articles I'd seen that were super relevant, liking pretty much every comment anyone made, getting stuck into every conversation . . . It was full on but it definitely worked; people got a sense of what the group was about. It also meant that existing group members would behave and interact in the kind of way that I was, which in turn helped new members to behave and interact in a way that existing members were, etc. As the group admin and owner, you really trickle down your values and aims for the group through your own posts and contributions. There's also nothing worse than a Facebook group with an absent "host" – you really have to be there at the forefront of the thing, driving the conversation forward. Having said that, now it's up and running the group is relatively straightforward to manage and is kind of running itself, so while I comment and interact when I can or it's relevant to do so, I'm less omnipresent than I once was.'

— I also love **Soulful pr: tips & advice for promoting your business,** which is led by PR guru Janet Murray. Janet posts loads of PR tips and links to her podcast and blog posts, but also gives opportunities for others to shout about what they're doing. She has over 12,000 members.

- **The No1 Freelance Ladies' Buddy Agency** is great if journalism or PR is your thing. Each Friday you can write pitch ideas and see if anyone would be up for publishing your article. Also, there are often requests for people who might like to appear on an ITV *Good Morning Britain* debate, or to speak on radio about something topical.

- As well as potentially starting a group, **join other Facebook groups** and engage with people's posts, as well as adding your own. It's about becoming part of a community, and gradually you'll find yourself new fans and so potential clients. Supporting other people will never harm your brand and will often act massively in your favour.

● ●

Instagram

Sarah Akwisombe (@sarahakwisombe; 22k+ followers) shares her top three tips for growing a big following on Instagram:

1. **Provide value.** So often I see people creating accounts that are purely there to have people fawn over them. I'm not saying that doesn't work but it only works for a very select few. The rest of us normal people need to actually add value to other people's lives in order to grow a following.

2. **Be authentic.** Don't do shit just for the gram, it's desperate and people can tell.

3. You need to **communicate your values** instantly in your visual aesthetic, so work on creating a strong brand look and feel.

— **Tag people in your posts** to get their attention. Don't do it too often, as it can be annoying to be tagged all the time and feel a bit 'try hard' but occasionally, it's fine – as long as it's relevant to them.

— **Big up other mothers.** Giving other mums a shout-out or virtual pat on the back will not lose you followers, on the contrary. Instagram is potentially an amazing platform for networking but you need to give support, as well as asking for it. Be generous.

- **Ask your followers questions.** Post a dilemma, or an achievement, and ask if they've felt similar or if it resonates with them. If I see a question about baby sleep, for instance, I find it hard not to respond because it's something I've obsessed over for so long.

- **Micro-blogging** (posting mini stories on Instagram) helps you to build an online persona. If you're comfortable with it, reveal something about yourself. People want to know the woman behind the logo and handle.

- The images are obviously very important on Instagram, and developing your own style: all black-and-white photos, or circular images (you can do this using an app like Frame Swagg to re-frame your photos before you upload them, look at @ihavethisthingwithvintage for inspiration), but **the captions matter, too.** Make them funny, captivating, honest, useful or informative. Choose your tone.

Sarah Turner (@theunmumsymum; 300k+ followers), says: 'Instagram, for me, came later and I almost didn't bother, assuming it would be the wrong platform for somebody who takes blurry pictures and has never once attempted a 'flat lay'. I was proven wrong, though, and I actually now use Instagram more than Facebook, though some content is duplicated across the two.'

Coral Atkinson, founder of Velveteen Babies (@ velveteen_babies; 72k+ followers) shares three tips for Instagram:

1. I definitely think that **consistency has a lot to do with creating a really clear branding message** on the Instagram feed which will draw people in. It might seem callous, but we are visual creatures and you only get a couple of seconds before someone moves away or decides to click 'follow'. Just straightening your image if it's a bit wonky, lightening an image if it's a bit dark, cast aside blurry captures, and use VSCO, A Color Story or Photoshop PS Express (a free phone app) to gently edit. There are tons of really great guides online for basic editing skills. Equally, some of the 'real' feeds that aren't visually edited are made popular by the captions, so think clearly about what you will be using Instagram for, as you'll find that different people are drawn to different things.

If you're more of a wordsmith, conjure up conversational posts and make sure you follow and interact with similar feeds.

2. **Use 'Stories' and captions to be real and show the world who you are.** I'm very honest in my personal account captions and Stories and I'm not afraid to be vulnerable and honest. I think the most vulnerable posts always get loads of engagement and are relatable to others, so it's totally fine to just be yourself. Equally, I know some posts won't do as well for 'likes' but will enhance the look of my feed and I don't always want to be vulnerable, so it is a balance! I also keep my business account relatable by frequently posting a bit of information about myself and making clear that although I am very fortunate to have a large following, my business is just 'me' and not a big corporate team. I muster up the courage to chat on Stories on both feeds, rather than hiding away, which always has a really positive response.

3. **Make meaningful conversation in captions and on other people's posts.**

Instagram is about community, not just quickly posting a picture then 'running'. The more you put into it, the more you'll get out of it. Commenting on posts that inspire you or that ask others' opinions is a great way to get noticed and the more you do it, the more response you'll get when you do post yourself. Ask for advice – people love to give it – but when starting out, spend more time interacting on other people's posts than waiting around for people to come to you.

Anna Jones says, 'My following has grown very organically. I share a lot of recipe content, which is valuable content, rather than "this is how I'm feeling" or a picture of a tree. I love that stuff too, but you have to find your value in the crazy realm of social media. For me, that's the stuff that goes on in my brain to do with food. What can you bring that not that many other people can? I try to have a level of honesty. My stuff isn't deeply personal but it is the food I make at home. Also, keep consistent with the look of the images. Especially in food, art and design – people expect a type of picture from me and when I break that it doesn't get as much interaction.'

Twitter

Twitter can be great for connecting with journalists and editors. Seek them out, follow them and check out their #journorequests – see who they're looking to interview, feature or what articles they want to commission. And make contact. If they follow you back, you can send a DM (direct message). If not, be brave and @ mention them. Remember, things move very quickly on Twitter. Unless your tweet is retweeted, or liked, it will disappear from people's feeds in moments, so no one will notice if your request to connect with a journalist is ignored.

Emma Simpson was a broadcast journalist for ITN. After having her two sons, now school-aged, she re-trained through Digital Mums and now manages the social media account of small businesses around school pick-ups. These are her suggestions for starting out on Twitter:

— **Follow other accounts in your field.** That can include individuals – influencers – as well as related publications and businesses. If you're a personal trainer, follow health and wellbeing magazines, other trainers who have a big following, businesses offering products who might want to collaborate with you.

— **Create lists.** This is a feature in Twitter. It allows you to group people together, for instance: journalists in your field could be in one group, influencers in another. This helps you to see what they're doing, saying and tweeting about without having to filter through the main feed.

— You want to **build a community,** so don't just tweet about yourself and your work. Big up other people, link to their articles – your tweets should be approximately 30 per cent about you and 70 per cent about other people, businesses, ideas, studies. Discuss developments in your field.

— The aim should be to **put out 10 tweets a day,** but that's a lot for someone starting out. So maybe aim for four at first: one about you, three promoting other people doing interesting stuff that relates to your work. Two hours a week on Twitter might be a good place to start: one scheduling tweets, one hour engaging with other people's tweets.

- **Develop a voice.** Become an expert. Be the person who has an interesting take on your profession. Then start and be part of other conversations. When you have some followers, you could arrange a live Twitter chat: inviting people to join you at 9 a.m. on Monday, for example, to discuss a topical issue. You put out questions, and ask people to answer them, @ mentioning you and including a hashtag that you've created on the topic.

- **Twitter is great for developing relationships with industry people.** If you respond to a tweet, this may be acknowledged with a 'like' or response. It's opened up communication between people starting out and people who are at the top of their game.

- As with the other platforms, **engage as much as possible.** Retweet other people's tweets, if they're talking about something interesting in your field. Respond to what they've said. Share your own articles and other people's – again, being generous in this way will make people warm to you.

Social media bios

Across all social media there will be space for a bio. This is somewhere for people to read more about who you are and what you do. Some people write clever copy, while others stick to explaining what they do in simple terms. I'd opt for the latter. If you're going to be using your social media channels to find new clients and drum up business, a cryptic paragraph won't cut it. This is your first impression, so you'll want to make a good one. Stick in anything impressive – any awards, recognition, perhaps a quote about your work from someone you respect. But if you're not quite there yet, stick to a simple explanation about what you do, and what you can offer – e.g. Helen Jones, freelance social media manager with a specialist knowledge of interior design. Available for short- and long-term management of your social channels. Get in touch: helen@helenjones.com.

Plan your posts in advance

With all your social media accounts, it can help to schedule content in advance. I use Hootsuite, but

Buffer is also popular, as is Planoly (for Instagram). You can write posts, add images and decide when you'd like the post to go out. Then check the stats: which posts have garnered the most likes or comments? Can you do more like that? What time did the post go out? When are people in your industry most active on social media? Check, test and then refine so that all your posts are engaging and going out when there are people online to see them. That said, it can be beneficial to post as and when the idea/inspiration strikes. Candice Brathwaite says: 'While many social influencers would disagree, I'm not 100 per cent sold on pre-planning my online content. To free up some headspace, I do a combination of both – this allows me to keep it real as I can post on the fly but also have images, blog posts and videos to share on days when I'm too busy/sick/tired or usually all three!'

How much time to spend on social

On how much time to dedicate to social media, Sarah Turner says: 'In the early days of the blog I dedicated very little time to social media – probably no more than ten minutes a day! Nowadays, it's more like an hour a day and, if I'm honest, quite often more!' You might like to spend an hour a day on social media, or three hours a week. In time, you'll work out your own rhythm.

To finish this section, here's some sound advice from Sarah: 'My advice for anyone who wants to grow a social media following is to ignore every single tip, trick and "best practice" you've been told is the formula for a successful social media presence and go your own way. On paper, I probably did (and still do!) everything wrong but it hasn't done me any harm. Also, never try and imitate somebody else. If it's not your natural voice it will feel awkward and you'll never be able to keep up the pretence.'

• •

Don't compare yourself to others

Steph Douglas says: 'Don't waste your energy on what everyone around you is doing. If you're really clear on your own idea and plan, stay focused. Someone else will have different circumstances, finances, childcare, plans, etc. Social media is a brilliant tool but can be terrible for seeing how well everyone else is supposedly doing. Use it to remind you to stay on your path and plough on, but not to try and compete against.'

Cherry Healey has similar advice. She says that it's natural to make certain comparisons – especially when we're presented with seemingly perfect lives on social media – but remember that everyone finds things tricky and faces challenges at least some of the time. 'Never compare yourself to other people,' she says, 'because it might look like everything's going so well, but then tomorrow they'll be having a little cry.' And that won't necessarily be documented on their Instagram grid.

7
Blogging and SEO

53 per cent of marketers say blogging is their top content marketing priority.[1]

When I finished my English BA, aged 22, I moved to Hackney and decided I was going to be a journalist. I sent out dozens of emails to local papers asking for a job. I couldn't believe it when none of them said yes. Most didn't even respond. I then contacted a local Hackney paper that was just starting up, and offered to write articles for free. At last, I got a 'yes'. I went out in east London interviewing artists and musicians and writing it up for the newspaper (and worked on the door of a nightclub to fund it). It was the start of online journalism, so the articles all went on the website but I was more excited about the print paper. I remember feeling exuberant on seeing my first front-page article when the paper came through the door.

However, I also wanted to write about things that weren't suitable for this newspaper: conversations I'd had, or exhibitions I'd been to that weren't in Hackney, or feminist books I was reading. So I started a blog. The word 'blog' had only been around for a few years. In fact, when I set up 'Annie Loves', I didn't know anyone else who was blogging. Over time, I developed a following. I'd write a post, add a picture (downloaded illegally from another website – I was yet to learn about copyright infringement) and publish it on my blogger-hosted blog. I'd then share it on Facebook and because this was before the sophisticated algorithm system had been set up, and before sponsored posts existed, everyone I was friends with would see it on their feed. Back then, I had about 1000 friends, so word spread and anyone who liked reading my musings would then look out for these posts.

The following year, I started a journalism MA and in one of the first lessons the teacher said: who has a blog? Only two of us – out of 30 – raised our hands. We were told that as journalists, we should be writing all the time, particularly online, as this course had an online focus. I continued blogging, and soon had a few hundred people visiting my website every day. I liked watching the view-counter on the front page of my blog go up but never even considered monetising it. In fact, a friend once asked what I was doing for work, if I was still blogging, if that was my job – and I laughed. I didn't realise this was something people could do. At the time, in 2008, there weren't many of us around. No one knew, back then, that in 10 years' time, blogging would become the must-have for every business.

Now most businesses do have a blog. As a freelancer, you can incorporate one into your website. It can be called the 'news' section, or 'journal' – whatever feels right for you and your work. But it's vital for SEO (meaning: if you want your website to sit at the top of Google search). Google loves fresh content, so if there's one website with a portfolio that occasionally has new pieces of work added to it, and another with a similar portfolio section but also a blog that has a weekly entry discussing a topical matter within the industry or reviewing a new product, it will push that second website up in its ratings. Also, blogs are a great way to keep 'keywords' moving around your website (more on this below).

You may not feel like a natural writer. You might have a fear of putting your writing out on the internet. But a blog will add huge value to your website and business. Many 'mumpreneurs' start with a blog – for example, Steph Douglas and Sarah Turner. Starting a blog is a way of gaining new followers, people who share your interests or like the way you talk (write) about your subject. And down the line this can be monetised – if you wish. Otherwise, it can sit along-side your other work, on your website, and get more people interested in the services you offer.

For Steph Douglas, this is exactly how her blog came about.

'I had the idea for the business in 2010 when Buster, my son, was born and I received eight bunches of flowers. I thought it was mad that the go-to gift for new mums was another thing to care for when they're doing more caring than they've ever done in their lives. I returned to work a year later and then got pregnant with my daughter, Mabel. During that time it became clearer in my mind that new mums need some TLC. It wasn't until I returned to work again when she was one that I started to think properly about turning this idea into a business.

'I started the blog at the start of 2014 as a kind of stepping stone. I'd had the idea for Don't Buy Her Flowers and initially it was aimed at new mums, so the blog was an honest account of motherhood and relationships with the idea that we're all in this together as none of us really knows what we're doing. It made sense that if people connected with the blog, they identified with the idea that was core to the business: that motherhood can be tricky and new mums deserve to be looked after.

'Starting a business felt like such a leap, so I gave myself the challenge of starting the blog to see if I could do it, and also knew I'd need to get involved with social media in order to market it and get to know our audience really well. I didn't monetise the blog because I didn't want it to feel anything but genuine. It did really well, with posts getting shared and thousands of views, and after a few months that had given me the confidence to start the business.

'On the night we launched Don't Buy Her Flowers, nine months later, in November 2014, our website crashed because everyone that was following the blog "got" what the business was about, were supportive and shared it far and wide. The blog now sits on our website and is great for adding new content and continuing to discuss things that are important to us and our customers, which all adds to clarifying what the brand is about. We now sell gift packages for many different reasons – bereavement, get well, birthdays and any occasion when someone wants to send some TLC. But central to everything we do is this idea of thoughtfulness that the business started with.'

For Emma Paton, her Finlay Fox blog was also a way of sharing her thoughts, not as an immediate business idea.

'I launched my blog a few years ago, while I was still working for Boden as a fashion buyer. I set it up as a bit of a hobby, a sideline where I could document my newfound passion after having my son and venturing into motherhood – sharing some fab kids' clothes and my newfound "mum style". I had a cool logo (courtesy of my brand creative neighbour) and nice modern feel to the blog to make it stand out. The main focus was always unisex and smaller independent brands and some original gifting ideas for design-conscious parents. The blog has evolved over the years and a second baby into focusing on motherhood, interiors and fashion.

'The blog was always intended to be an outlet or forum for expressing myself and my style and also something that could work longer term as a main job if it was successful. I also knew it would work well remotely if we moved outside of London, which is still the intention one day. My blog is now my main job as I wanted to be able to have the flexibility to do school pick-ups and drop-offs and support my son when he started school last year. I couldn't do this with my full-time 9–5 job. I love the flexibility it offers me around my family life, the people I've met and how every week can be so different.'

Emma Paton's top three tips for setting up and launching a blog are:

1. **Write about what you're passionate about,** as it's a lot of work and you need to have plenty of ideas. At the start it's likely that most of what you do will be written for free so you need to be really interested and committed to it.

2. **Be brave and put yourself out there.** Create a support network – contact other bloggers you like and introduce yourself or meet for a cuppa. Get support and advice from them – this is where most of my blogger knowledge has come from. Help champion each other and have someone to turn to when you have a question. Get business cards made and network like crazy!

3. **Trial and error.** Blogs can be an overnight success if you're very lucky but for most of us it is a slow-burner that does take time to build and grow organically. It is worth trying out a few different ideas to see what gets a good reaction and be ready to adapt and change if needs be – while remaining true to yourself and authentic.

And Emma Paton's top tips for making money from a blog are:

1. **Email a whole host of PR companies and brands** to introduce yourself and give examples of relevant pieces you've already written or mentioned them in. Even if you only get a few responses you have some good contacts to work with. Propose ideas for collaborating. They might want to know your analytics – for example, your engagement rate on Instagram and monthly blog hits.

2. **Know your worth and don't be afraid to be cheeky.** Understand the value of your influence, believe in what you have created and built up, and feel free to say no if someone can't pay you for a job. Niche bloggers can charge more. Tier pricing for different levels of work is good. Also, follow up emails and chase if you don't get a response.

3. **Make sure that any paid work still sits in line with your business ethos.** Think about what your brand values are. You want your work to be successful and building long-term relationships with the right, relevant brands

who pay is a good way to have consistent paid work.

Before starting a blog, you'll need to answer these questions:

— **What will my blog offer?** Will it be informative, offer solutions, be creative, insightful, analytical or feature reviews?

— **What will my tone be?** Academic, informal, funny, feminist, etc.?

— **How often will I post?** Daily, weekly, monthly? Decide, and stick to this – your readers will like this and so will search engines.

— **What length will my posts be?** 300 words is the minimum for SEO, 500–800 is a readable length, longer articles of 1000–3000 words will do well, if the content is captivating and people stay to read the whole piece.

You should see the blog as an important part of your work, as it can lead to new business. When the big news broadcasters are looking for 'experts' to come in and discuss a news story, they'll google to see if anyone's written a blog post on this particular topic. You want to be the person whose blog they come across, so you can speak live on air and then become the go-to for all related news items. For instance, BBC Radio 5's Jeremy Vine show wanted to do a piece on colic. I'd written a blog post about it so they contacted me and asked me to come on air to discuss the condition. I did, and was introduced as Annie Ridout, founder of The Early Hour. That got me a load of hits on my website, and I'm now down on their books as someone who can come on to talk about parenting issues. If you're a freelance beautician, you want to be producing content on your blog on this subject – make-up trends, cosmetics, beauty treatments – so that when a news story pops up, or someone's making a documentary about it, they come straight to you for an interview.

SEO tricks and tips

I've mentioned SEO (search engine optimisation) a few times already. It's a bit of a non-phrase until you're producing content online and wondering why no one is reading it. And then you might just become a bit obsessed, as I have. Google ranks your website in terms of how relevant the content/information is and how many people are visiting it. So, put very simply:

create relevant articles, covering topics within your field of expertise, but you then need to fix the SEO so that people actually read those articles. Having spent many an hour researching 'how to get more people on my website' I've become something of an SEO expert, so let me save you a lot of time and share everything I've learned about how to get loads of people reading your blog.

i. SEO is Google

Don't waste time on Yahoo, Bing or any other search engines, as 95 per cent of all searches in the EU are via Google. So you want to work out how to rise in the Google search engine and forget the others. But SEO is getting harder. When searching something on Google, you'll notice the website at the top of the list often says 'ad'. That's because someone's paid to be in that top spot. Similarly, the links down the right-hand side are paid-for. So even if your website has the most traffic and best SEO, another website can pay to appear above you. This demeans work you might be doing to improve your SEO but it's still worth working hard to move up the rankings. Although most people don't realise those top links are advertised rather than the websites with the best credentials, others do and skip straight down past the advertised sites.

ii. Track everything

Install Google analytics, if you haven't already, because this will tell you where your readers are coming from (whether it's from Facebook, a Google search, Twitter or somewhere else). Once they arrive at your site, what are they clicking on? Are they going straight to the shop, or the blog? Are they reading your 'about' section (if so, make sure it's up-to-date). Know who's coming and how they're using your site.

iii. Keyword research

Do keyword research. It's important to know which keywords you're optimising for (or, in other words, what people are typing into Google before coming across your site). You can do this using Google analytics, Moz (https://moz.com/) or Alexa (alexa.com/siteinfo). These sites will tell you exactly which search terms are leading people to your site. You can also find out which search terms are leading people to your competitors' sites – so do. And then nick them. If there's a term that is sending a whole load of traffic their way, and your product is similar, make sure you embed that term in your copy and across your site, too.

iv. Choose your keywords

What keywords do you want people to use so that they find your site? For The Early Hour, I'd like people to type 'early', 'parenting', 'mornings', 'up early', 'lifestyle articles' into Google and for my site to come up first. Choose the best keywords for your website and make sure you use them a lot in articles or blog posts, on the 'about' page. Everywhere. The subject of your blog posts should be related to your field of work so that it appeals to your target audience. If you're an illustrator, write blog posts about other illustrators, the art world, tips on how to draw. If you're a yoga teacher, write about wellbeing, or yoga routines to try at home. If you're a psychotherapist, offer tips for reducing anxiety in the workplace, or discuss the body–mind connection.

v. Type ahead

One trick is to start typing the search term you think should be associated with your site and see what comes up. Those are the top most-searched-for terms, I might type 'parenting' or 'early'. Whatever the top searches are signal how people look for content surrounding these subjects. But make sure that you differentiate between the top searches in a different colour, as these will be sites you've searched for yourself. It's the ones below that matter.

vi. Linking

You need to be including outbound links in your website – for instance, linking to other websites you like. And, more importantly, you want other sites to be linking back to you. If you have loads of links from small businesses, Google will favour your site. And if you have links from reputable websites (the BBC, academic sites, government sites) this is even better. How to get those links? It requires imagination and determination. You can email those places and tell them about your business. Follow them on social media and keep an eye on updates (perhaps they're looking to feature a business like yours?). Or write guest posts for other sites, which will include a link to yours.

And what do you need those links to say? Yeah, it's not as simple as just getting a link. You need the copy that links through to be relevant so that Google makes the connection. For instance, for The Early Hour, I'd need another site to say something like: The Early Hour publishes articles early in the morning, at 5 a.m. So Google will pick up the 'early in the morning' and 'articles' and associate it with theearlyhour.com. Don't be tempted to pay for links to your website, Google will see that you've done this and penalise you, pushing you down the rankings.

Another tip is to link within your own site – internal links; it connects all your content together. A blog post about healthy smoothies to drink first thing in the morning could link to another you wrote about herbal teas to wake you up. It keeps readers on your website and each post is boosted in the rankings by the other.

vii. Use an SEO plugin

If your site is hosted on WordPress, you can install the Yoast plugin, which guides you through the steps required to optimise each article you put up, to ensure it has the best chance of featuring high up on Google. I use it, and it's great.

To summarise:

— **Pick the right keywords**

— **Use them lots within your site**

— **Link to other sites and get them to link to you**

— **Link internally**

— **Get an SEO plugin**

● ●

Writing for online

— **Write a header** that encompasses what the post is about. So if I'm writing a blog post on 'colic' that's the most important term and should be in my header, e.g. Is colic the reason my baby cries all evening? But also, get creative. Write something that makes people want to read the post, like: There's only one cure for colic. This is it.

— **This keyword should then be used throughout** your post. In the introduction

– the first paragraph – use it again, e.g. As a newborn baby, my daughter suffered with colic. In this article, I'll discuss how it manifested and the tricks I discovered for relieving the symptoms.

— In the **blog post URL** (the web address), make sure the keyword appears.

— **Create subheadings within the piece,** to break up the content. The main header is called the H1. Within the copy, you can have H2 headers (they are just a bit smaller than the header at the top), H3 – smaller again – and then H4, H5, H6. On a standard WordPress blog, the options for subheadings will be in the toolbar, at the top of the post, under the drop-down menu that says 'paragraph'. These headers are picked up by Google, so include that keyword (e.g. colic) again in at least one of them.

— For the web, your **paragraphs should be short** – maybe three lines each.

— **Look at your competitors** and borrow ideas for how they're creating good, sharable content. But don't steal their copy, and avoid duplicating content – even if you've been given permission. Google wants original content, not carbon copies.

— If you write a guide that teaches people how to do something, they are more likely to share it. **Informative copy always does well.** That's why headers which use things like: '5 ways to get fussy eaters to love greens' do well; it appeals to almost all parents, and if a friend says: my kid won't eat her vegetables, another parent will send a link to this piece. Also, the number makes it sound digestible – it's not a long, drawn-out article, it's a snappy one, broken down into bitesize chunks.

— **Interview other people in your field.** This is advantageous for a few reasons: the content will likely appeal to your readers, it shows that you're supportive rather than competitive, and they will hopefully share the interview on their own social channels which will put you in front of a load more potential fans.

— Work out **when to publish your posts.** With The Early Hour, I publish content at 5 a.m., for parents who are up early. If your readers are more likely to read on their lunch break, or late at night, put it out then. This might require some trial and error to get the optimum timing.

— **Proofread** before hitting 'publish'. Copy that's full of typos and mis-spelled words is unprofessional; it immediately puts me off a business or product if I spot copy errors.

• •

Images for web

Use your own photographs, ideally, or photos from a website like Unsplash, where you can download them for free and use them legally. Save the photo on your desktop with your keyword. When you upload it, make the 'title' of the photo the same as your blog post title. This means it will pop up in Google images when someone types in your keyword, and they'll be led through to your article.

All of this might sound daunting, particularly if you're not a keen writer, but you'll soon get into it. If it takes you longer to write and you're not sure how to fit it into your work schedule, you could always stockpile content during quiet periods. Publishing blog posts at regular intervals (weekly, monthly, etc.) doesn't have to mean writing them then. They can be written up in advance, when you have more time, and stored in drafts, so that you can continue publishing during busier periods, when your focus is on another part of the business.

In the lead-up to my son's birth, I stockpiled three months' worth of articles so that I could still put out one a day when he was tiny. When he was older, I realised that I had a constant underlying stress from getting an article written, edited, uploaded and scheduled to go out every day, as well as the associated social media posts. So I stopped. I reduced it to one article a week. I can't tell you how relieved I felt. Slowing down The Early Hour content allowed me to focus on other areas of my career – the stuff I really love doing – like writing for other websites. And then I got this book deal. It's like I'd created space in my life for it. Don't be afraid to reassess and make changes.

8

PR: the best person to do it is YOU

PR, put simply, is spreading the word about you and your work, via the media. So if you're selling a service or product, you want all the big news desks, magazines and broadcasters to be writing and talking about it so that you can reach a huge audience – and get new customers or clients. When you're starting out, no one will know what you have to offer. Therefore, you'll need to become accustomed to blowing your own trumpet. Tell everyone what you're doing. And be proud. Become a salesperson and sell yourself. I didn't like doing this at first, I thought: no one cares about me and my work. But over time, I realised that actually some people did care. What I was writing about resonated with people. And so I learned to shout about it – in real life, and on social media.

Being a writer helped. When I launched The Early Hour, I wanted links to my website from the *Guardian*, *The Times* – all the big websites. I knew this would be good for SEO (getting higher in the Google searches), but I also wanted any parents who read the article to become a reader of my website, too. So I set out on a mission to get as much coverage as possible. I soon realised that this would benefit me, and The Early Hour, but that I would also be helping journalists and editors who are always on the lookout for new content.

But what if writing isn't your first craft? Anna Jones started out as a chef and later launched her own brand, initially doing cookbooks. When she was later offered the opportunity to write a column for the *Guardian*, she couldn't turn it down, but she found these 2500-word articles nervewracking to write. 'I felt confident writing in recipe format. I've always felt a clear way of communicating that – I know what's happening with my hands; I know the point at which caramel turns from pale to burned, so describing that came naturally.' But the longer form pieces – her column, or the introductions to her books – were harder. And yet it was such a good PR opportunity, as everyone who read and liked her column would then buy her books, so she persevered, and now the anxiety she once felt about writing these pieces has subsided.

• •

Your story

In order to get journalists and editors interested in you, you'll need to develop your 'story'. This is your journey, and what makes you interesting and worth speaking to. For me, it was about setting up The Early Hour after losing my job, and how I'd made it work while looking after my baby. So any time someone was looking to speak to a new mother, a woman who'd experienced maternity discrimination, freelancing parents or anything else that related to my 'story', I'd offer to be interviewed, and soon journalists were approaching me. For Anna Jones, it was about breaking into vegetarianism at a time when it wasn't yet 'on trend'. The Step Up Club founders, Alice Olins and Phanella Mayall Fine, are often featured in women's mags like *Grazia*, or in the *Telegraph*. Their 'story' is that they are at the forefront of a new movement; teaching women (particularly mothers) how to become badass at running their own businesses, through their courses and events.

Put yourself forward

A month after launching, I was on Twitter – I'd started following all the journalists and editors I liked – and came across a request from a *Sunday Times* journalist for a mother who'd be willing to talk about the ridiculously high childcare costs in the UK. I put myself forward, and this led to an interview in the *Sunday Times*, a photographer coming to my house to take the main photo for the article, and mentions of The Early Hour. The piece appeared under both 'news' and 'money'. Online and in print. That got me new followers, and I could link through from my website, in the About section, which was a great endorsement (in my readers' eyes, as well as Google's).

I soon discovered the 'journorequest' hashtag. If you type #journorequest into Twitter, journalists looking to interview people for an article they're writing often use this hashtag so their requests all appear in a neat line. If any are relevant to you, you can send an email saying you'd love to be interviewed. When the *Guardian* were looking for women to talk about sexual harassment in the workplace, I contacted the journalist, offering to share my experience. My name and website appeared in the article. This was picked up by the BBC and led to a TV appearance and to talking on radio. I stayed in contact with that *Guardian* journalist – who also happened to be an editor – and pitched an idea to her (via Twitter, private messages). This resulted in me writing an article for the *Guardian* about setting up The Early Hour.

But be sure to jump at these opportunities. Journalists and editors are busy people; if they receive one reply to a callout on Twitter immediately and another two days later, which interviewee are they going to go with? I'm often surprised by how slack people are when it comes to making use of free PR. If I'm looking for people to interview for The Early Hour, which reaches over 100,000 parents every month across the website and social media channels, I'll put a callout on social media. The emails will flow in, I'll then respond – possibly send some interview questions – and quite often, won't hear back. Or not for a few weeks. By then, I've moved on to the next story or interview series. So be quick, be efficient and remember that people are busy and most likely won't chase you unless your story is exceptionally unique and exciting.

• •

Aim high

In your wildest dreams, who would be writing about you and what would they say? If what you'd love is for a *Guardian* women's editor to be endorsing your products or services – contact them. Tell them about you and your work. Share your story. Aim high. And if you don't hear back, move to your second-biggest dream, in terms of coverage. I had a chat with someone recently who wanted to write about travel with a special needs child. She was writing a blog but I thought this could make a really good column for the *Guardian*. She didn't believe this was possible, but of course it is. Editors are looking for good stories, new ideas and people who can write, or will make an interesting interviewee.

Gorkana

Sign up to gorkana.com and request the daily email with news about newly appointed positions within journalism. I get this every morning and it includes a list of editors and journalists who've moved into a new role or started working at a different publication. This means they'll be on the lookout for new stories in this field, so I contact them congratulating them on the new position and then pitch my story idea. Even if you're not able to pitch immediately, create a 'contacts' list and add their name and email addresses to it. You can come back to it later, when you have a great idea for an article and need to get in touch with the editor of a specific section.

•••••••••••••••••••••••••••••

Be helpful

If you're being interviewed by a journalist about your work and they're looking for others to interview too, give them ideas. Put them in touch with people you know. It doesn't mean they won't use your interview, but it does mean that they'll remember you as someone helpful and efficient and they'll come back to you next time they're writing about this same subject. I was invited to talk at *Stylist* Live and the event organiser, Debbie, asked if I could think of any other women who would make good speakers. I spent an hour researching and sent her a list. One of my suggestions was Pippa Murray, the founder of Pip & Nut peanut butter, who I'd interviewed for The Early Hour. Debbie obviously liked this idea, as Pippa ended up speaking at the event. I'm now in talks with Debbie about speaking at the next *Stylist* Live event. Be helpful. It will never do you any harm.

How to contact editors and journalists

So you've decided you'd like to be featured in two national newspapers and three women's magazines, now what? Well, you have to make contact with the right people. National news websites will have various sections – women, tech, news, health, etc. Where do you and your work fit in? With The Early Hour, I aim for Family, Women and Opinion (as I have one, on everything parenting-related). Next, find out who the editor of that section is, via Google. Follow them on Twitter. If their email address isn't in their bio, again, google it. You'll usually come across it. If you don't, phone the main desk and request it. Or just look at the usual format for email addresses, for instance at the *Guardian*, the email format is: Firstname.lastname@theguardian.com.

Write an email introducing yourself. Keep it brief, editors are busy people. Make sure the subject line is captivating. I secured an interview with Arianna Huffington by emailing with the following subject line:

Sleep. Sleep. Sleep. Sleep. Sleep. Sleep. Sleep.

At the time, she was doing a massive campaign on sleep and this caught her attention. Ideally, editors will be looking for stories associated with existing news stories. So if the government announce changes to paternity pay for freelancers, that's a great time to pitch a story about how you and your husband – a fellow freelancer – have decided to take shared parental leave because of this change in law. Editors will jump at this, as they'll be looking for case studies. You can then write up your story, with a mention about your freelance work: Annie Ridout, freelance journalist, has decided to take Shared Parental Leave following the change in legislation.

If it's a newsy story that you're pitching, get in contact as soon as the new story breaks. You could pitch a *Guardian* Opinion article if you see a news story and have very strong views on it, perhaps due to your own experience. So if I see anything about parenting young children in the news, I'll start pitching article ideas. Journalist Robyn Wilder says: 'I find that if I scour the news at night for hooks I can get pitches into morning editorial meetings.' This is a great idea. Find the news story, pitch your angle first thing in the morning before the editors and journalists gather to discuss how they'll be covering the day's stories.

If your story isn't attached to a current news story – it's just about you and your business or services – I find the best time to pitch is around mid-morning on a Tuesday. Manic Monday has passed, the emails have been filtered through. First thing in the morning is always hectic. The end of the day is when people are winding down, or leaving early to collect the kids. Catch them in the mid-morning calm. Once you've pitched your article or interview idea, following up a few days later with a simple: Just wondered if you've had a chance to read the email I sent over, about writing an article for you on how I've built a freelance career around looking after my four kids full-time? Most editors won't respond, at least initially. Of those who do, most will say no. But keep going: if it's a good story, someone will bite. You'll refine your pitching skills over time.

Press releases are out

Writing a long, detailed press release with a series of images is – in my opinion and experience – outdated. Journalists and editors don't have time to open everyone's attachments. What they want is an email written directly to them, explaining the article or interview idea and why it's current or going to get loads of hits on their website. Imagine if you were an editor, receiving hundreds of emails a day from people who want to be featured in their publication, would you open attachments and read through it all? No, probably not. But if someone addressed you directly, with a story or idea that was going to capture people's imaginations – and a brilliant photograph – you'd be in. Forget the press release. Save yourself time, and give editors' and journalists' mailboxes a break from the generic mail-outs.

• •

Set Google alerts

If you set Google alerts, you'll receive an email with any relevant news stories each morning. I have Google alerts set so that any news stories about mornings, parenting and women come straight through to my inbox. Then I can filter these and see if I can write an article about any of these stories. You can also just do a quick Google search on the mornings you're working. Type in a search term that relates to you and your work and check the 'news' results. I also do this when looking for stories for BabyCentre, who I write regular blog posts for, googling 'baby', 'mother', 'motherhood', 'family' to get ideas of news stories that I can share my opinion on for the BabyCentre blog.

Make life easier for editors

If an editor agrees to you writing an article, or a journalist decides to interview you, make life easy for them. Stick to the word count you've agreed, proof your copy so that there are no errors (get someone else to, as well) and always send an image of you or your product. It saves them having to ask for one. Ensure it's high res, but small enough to be sent attached to an email. This means if they need a main image for the article, they'll use yours. This can be particularly beneficial if you're being interviewed alongside other freelancers, as the section about you will stand out more if it's your image at the top of the piece. I sent a high-quality photo of me when I was interviewed about being a female entrepreneur for the *Telegraph* and it was used as the main image. That meant every time the article was shared online, my photo was too, with a caption about me and my services underneath it.

Within the copy you're sending over (your interview answers), if you've linked to another website, hyperlink so that they don't have to find the link source. And hyperlink your social media handles, if you want them included in a bio – you do – because the editor might otherwise just leave them written out and people won't be able to click through directly. If you're not familiar with hyperlinking, it involves highlighting your website – e.g. theearlyhour.com, then pasting in the URL when prompted, e.g. http://theearlyhour.com – so that it will link through directly when the editor clicks it on theearlyhour.com.

Be likeable

A lot of my freelance journalism is commissioned, so rather than me pitching, an editor comes to me and asks if I can write something off the back of a news or celebrity story that's just broken. If I was unreliable or didn't proof my work properly, they wouldn't come knocking. Especially for online. *Stylist*, for example, have come to me twice asking if I can knock up an online piece in two hours. That includes research, interviews, writing, proofing. They then want to upload it straight to the web. If they have to fact-check and heavily proof or edit, it becomes a burden for them. Don't be a burden. Make their job easy.

Your own mailing list

You'll want to build your own mailing list and send out a regular newsletter about what's going on with you and your work. MailChimp is a useful website for this. It's free to create newsletters – using their templates – and to send them to up to 2000 subscribers. You can re-use the same template each week, just adding in new images and copy. Ask people if it's OK to sign them up to your mailing list – this is a legal, GDPR requirement – create a pop-up box on your website offering the opportunity to be added to it and tell people about your mailing list on social media. Grow this as big as you can, it's a great marketing tool. Imagine you have an offer for your customers or clients and can send it out to all of them at once. This is what mailing lists are for.

When starting out, it might be more realistic to aim for a monthly newsletter. If this goes well, and sends lots of people through to your website, shop or gets you new followers, you could consider doing a weekly round-up of recent events/products/news/competitions. It's about adding value to your customers – this is free content, being sent directly to their mailbox. If they like it, that's such a treat. Of course, if they don't, they'll unsubscribe. If this starts to happen regularly, re-think your approach. Maybe it needs to be more personal, or less personal. Perhaps it's a bit salesy or feels like it's asking too much of them. Ask people, via your social channels, what they think of your newsletter. Or ask them directly in a newsletter: I'd love to hear your thoughts about this weekly newsletter, what you'd like more or less of. Any pointers would be much appreciated.

Some of the newsletters I love receiving, and actually read, are from The Step Up Club (helping women succeed in business), Harriet Minter (full of freelance tips, advice and news. I love that she shares other people's articles and podcasts that might be of interest, they always are, to me) and Women Who (for creative working women, founded by Otegha Uwagba. It's genuinely helpful).

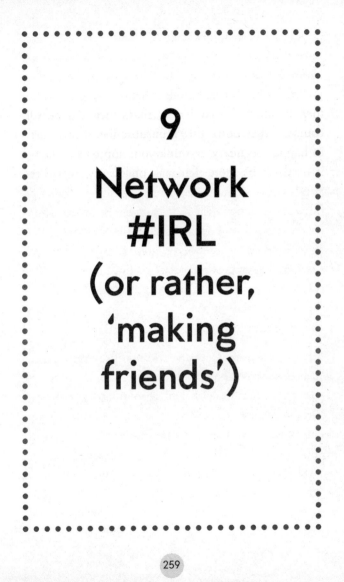

9
Network #IRL
(or rather, 'making friends')

A few years ago, I was at a blogging awards ceremony. There was lots of schmoozing and a young woman came up to introduce herself. She was polite and friendly and managed to tell me a fair bit about herself, while also asking what I did. After about five minutes, she said, 'OK, so nice meeting you, now I'm going to move around the room.' At the time, I thought it was quite smooth – she was being honest, while polite, about the fact that she was here for work. However, networking shouldn't just be about 'working the room'. In fact, it should be about making new friends. Because as soon as that woman danced off, that was the end of our relationship. I never spoke to her again, or followed her on social media or helped her in any way. Really, you want to be developing lasting relationships.

One of my most inspiring friendships, with Danielle Pender, came about because we had children the same age. We were at a playgroup and got talking: she didn't know anything about me, I didn't know anything about her. But her daughter had sat on my lap and passed me a book, and after laughing we got chatting. Back then, I was launching The Early Hour, so when we eventually got on to talking about work, and she mentioned *Riposte Magazine* – which

I'd heard of – I asked if she might be up for meeting for a coffee, as I'd love her advice on a few things. She kindly agreed, and we quickly became friends. It wasn't about networking, it was about building a friendship (though, over the years, she's also given me some brilliant help and advice).

Of course, you shouldn't start a conversation with: so, what do you do (thinking: and how can you help forward my career). You need to be open-minded, friendly and enquiring at all times. The man serving your morning coffee could be your next client. So could your kid's teacher at school. Show an interest in everyone, and you never know where it could lead. And if you get chatting to someone who's in the same line of work as you, don't see this as competition, see it as the potential for collaboration – she might have too many clients, and pass one on to you. You might have a big project come in and need another pair of hands. Also, it's always good to have people who are experts in the same field as you to brainstorm or share ideas with.

Stylist Bertie Bowen says it's important to be open-minded and talk to everyone. 'Reach out to those you admire who are in the same area of work you are in or want to be in,' she says. 'Talk to your neighbours, talk to that woman in your yoga class who seems cool, actually talk to everyone – you never know who is going to have advice or give you inspiration or know someone who could help you get a foot in the door.'

Jenny Scott, founder of Mothers Meetings and mum of three, shares her networking tips:

- Remember **everyone is in a similar position** to you. It may feel as though every mother in the room/playground/soft play centre knows each other, but they don't! And the chances are they feel just as scared and anxious as you do.

- **Be honest.** When you start a conversation, don't pretend you're anything but yourself. If you don't know what you're doing, or you're feeling exhausted and finding things hard as a mum, be open and tell people how you really feel. Nine times out of 10 they'll be relieved, and feeling exactly the same.

- **Ask questions.** It's always nice to find out about other people, pay an interest in who they are or what they do. You never know, you might have way more in common than you could have imagined.

- **Find out their social media handle** and rather than being a bit full-on at first by asking to meet up for a tea (though this may not be a problem for some), once you get home drop them a DM on Insta – all mums are on the lookout for new like-minded friends.

- Tea on Tuesdays? **Don't be afraid to host your very own get together** – put something on social media about meeting at a gallery or exhibition. You'll be surprised at how many people will be grateful for the opportunity to stimulate their 'baby brain'.

Alice Olins and Phanella Mayall Fine say, 'Networking is just conversations with a purpose. So many of us get hung up on the word "networking" (granted, there is some terrible jargon in career development circles), that we give up before we've even got going. Networking really isn't as scary as it's cracked up to be, especially in these digitally enhanced times, when we are able to hide behind an email, or Insta DM. Many of us fear real-life networking, so feel comforted by numbers if that's you.

'Also, don't put too much pressure on yourself to be out at every networking event going; even diehard networkers would balk at that. If you know you're more introverted, set your aims on the lower end of the scale: when you find yourself in a room full of unknown faces, just look to meet one new person. The more extroverted among us may thrive on holding court at every networking bash in the diary, but if that isn't you, that's OK.'

The Step Up Club's top five networking tips:

1. **Assess the network you already have.**
   Chances are, you've got a much bigger network than you give yourself credit for. What we like to do is draw a sort of Venn diagram of all the spheres of people that you know, then fill in the names once you have your framework in place. There are so many places that your network extends into: school, old friends, colleagues past and present, friends of friends, extended family, people you met while abroad, your mum group, gym buddies, the list is endless. It's a real networking confidence boost just seeing how many people you already know and being objective about where your network extends into.

2. **Don't fear the approach.** How do you feel when you receive an unexpected email from

a very old friend, or a friend of a friend who wants your help? We bet you feel flattered. Yes, it's scary sending out cold emails, but be comforted in the knowledge that, like you, other people enjoy the experience. OK, there might be one or two who never get back to you (nothing lost there then), but in the main, you're likely to receive an equally pleasant and helpful reply. See, making connections is just not as scary as it feels inside our heads?

3. **Learn to feel comfortable with an asymmetrical ask.** A what?! An asymmetrical ask is simple: it's the art of asking for something and having nothing to immediately offer in return. Men are great at this type of networking, mainly because they don't get so emotionally involved and are more comfortable with the transactional approach. We can learn from the way men network in this way. It really is fine for you to ask something of a work contact – any contact really – and not have something immediate to give them back. Remember, just because you don't have a nugget of advice/new business lead to give back at that exact moment, doesn't mean you won't

be able to return the favour sometime in the future.

4. **Network in stories.** If you want to be memorable, approach networking as a story-telling experience. As humans we remember in narrative, so make it easier for others to positively set you apart, by learning to tell your career journey, or your pitch as a lightly emotive story.

5. **The follow-up.** Networking is nothing if you don't follow up. Building a little black book of new contacts is all very well, but if you don't access those names you're not really networking at all. There are so many easy ways to touch base with the contacts in your extended network: drop them an email, share an interesting news feature on Facebook, invite them for an after-work drink, introduce them to someone you might think they'd like to know. Really, staying in touch with your network, keeping it as a live organism, is the root to career success.

Suzy Ashworth on making the 'right' friends:

'You may have heard the common adage that you are the sum of the five people you spend the most time with. Who are you spending your time with? People who believe in themselves, are embracing success, who are not afraid of acknowledging their ambitions? If you aren't, change your crew. The energy of momentum is a beautiful thing – when you see other people doing what you want to do and achieve around you. People who inspire you and you can learn from . . . it's amazing how quickly you start to shine like a light in your own arena.'

End note

End note

I'm not always organised. I don't always manage to be productive during my children's naps – sometimes I just scroll through Facebook for an hour. I love the idea of healthy, wholesome working-from-home lunches, but sometimes I just eat cheese and crackers while typing up an article. And I'm not always in work mode come 7 p.m. Like all parents, I get tired and need to just put my feet up in the evening. I have days where I feel so stressed, I cry. And then phone my mum. And then cry again. The freelance mum life isn't perfect, it's not the answer to all mum–work balance issues. Sometimes I think: why am I doing this? If I had full-time childcare, life would be easier and I'd be much richer. But then I remind myself that I'd lose out on being around while my children are young. I hope that this book has helped you to see that it's possible to work around family life – giving a bit to both, while also having (at least a small amount of) time for yourself.

I'd love to hear about you and your freelance journey. We can connect on Instagram: @annieridout, Twitter: @annieridout, or send me an email: annie@annieridout.com.

• •

UK co-working spaces with crèche

Bloomsbury Beginnings (pop-up): Tuesdays and Fridays, Kings Cross, London: bloomsburybeginnings.org

Creche and Co (pop-up): open Mondays, Walthamstow, London: @crecheandco on Twitter

Cuckooz Nest: Monday–Friday with crèche, 24-hour access for members, Clerkenwell, London: cuckooznest.co.uk

Desks & Daycare (coming soon): Truro/Falmouth in Cornwall

Entreprenursery: Monday–Friday, 9 a.m.–5 p.m., Shoreditch, London: entreprenursery.co.uk

Farm Work Play: Monday–Friday, 7 a.m.–7 p.m., between Whitstable and Faversham, Kent: farmworkplay.co.uk

Huckletree: Monday–Friday, three locations in London: White City, Shoreditch, Clerkenwell: huckletree.com

Impact Hub Birmingham: crèche open Mondays, Birmingham: birmingham.impacthub.net

Isel Co-Work Creche (weekly pop-up): Solihull and south Birmingham: iselworkcreche.co.uk

Let's Play Coworking (pop-up): open daily, The Jury's Inn, Oxford: letsplaycoworking.com/jurys-inn

More2Childcare: Monday–Friday, Greenwich, London: more2childcare.com

Mother House: various opening hours, Stroud, London and Dagenham, motherhousestudios.com

PlayPen: Monday and Thursday, Mile End, London: playpencowork.com

Third Door: Monday–Friday, Putney, London: third-door.com

V22 Early Years: Monday–Friday, Dalston, London: v22collection.com/early-years

Reference notes

Introduction

1 Kayte Jenkins, 'Exploring the UK Freelance Workforce in 2016', IPSE, February 2017 (www.ipse.co.uk). https://www.ipse.co.uk/uploads/assets/uploaded/de84 dfb7-283a-4c26-ba446f95f5547c1f.pdf

2 'Managing Pregnancy and Maternity in the Workplace', Equality and Human Rights Commission. www.equality humanrights.com/en/our-work/ managing-pregnancy-and-maternity-workplace

1: Getting started as a freelance mum

1 John Colapinto, 'Famous Names: Does It Matter What a Product Is Called?', *New Yorker*, 3 October 2011. www.newyorker.com/magazine/2011/10/03/ famous-names

2: Money

1 'Do Women Earn Less Than Men in the UK?', Full Fact, 16 November 2017. https://fullfact.org/ economy/UK_gender_pay_gap/

2   Danielle Richardson, 'Self-Employed: Tax-Allowable
    Expenses', *Which?*, April 2018. www.which.co.uk/
    money/tax/income-tax/income-tax-for-the-self-
    employed/self-employed-tax-allowable-expenses-
    ayj250c7672j

3   The Childcare Service, GOV.UK. https://childcare-
    support.tax.service.gov.uk/par/app/trialmessage

4   Helen Saxon and Wendy Alcock, 'Childcare Costs
    Help', MoneySavingExpert.com, updated 4 September
    2018. www.moneysavingexpert.com/family/childcare-
    costs/

5   'Income Tax Rates and Personal Allowances', GOV.
    UK. www.gov.uk/income-tax-rates

3: The daily routine

1   Hannah Martin, 'How to Work Cleverly Around
    Your Menstrual Cycle', 23 October 2014.
    www.talentedladiesclub.com/articles/work-cleverly-
    around-menstrual-cycle/

4: The pram in the hall

1   'Average Childcare Costs', Money Advice Service.
    www.moneyadviceservice.org.uk/en/articles/childcare-
    costs

2   'Help Paying for Childcare', GOV.UK. www.gov.uk/
    help-with-childcare-costs/free-childcare-and-
    education-for-2-to-4-year-olds

3   'Childminders', BabyCentre. www.babycentre.co.uk/
    a537540/childminders

4 'Nannies', BabyCentre. www.babycentre.co.uk/a5375
   48/nannies

5: Fake it till you make it

1 Jon Vale, 'Gender Pay Gap: Women Hold Just 12%
   of Jobs Paying £150,000 or More', *Independent*,
   20 January 2017. www.independent.co.uk/news/
   business/news/women-jobs-careers-12-per-cent-jobs-
   paying-150000-per-year-income-gender-pay-gap-
   equality-a7537306.html

6: How to stand out on social media

1 Simon Kemp, 'Special Reports: Digital in 2016',
   We Are Social, 27 January 2016. https://wearesocial.
   com/uk/special-reports/digital-in-2016

2 Jeff Dunn, 'Facebook Totally Dominates the List of
   Most Popular Social Media Apps', Business Insider,
   27 July 2017. http://uk.businessinsider.com/facebook-
   dominates-most-popular-social-media-apps-
   chart-2017-7

7: Blogging and SEO

1 'The Ultimate List of Marketing Statistics for 2018',
   HubSpot. https://www.hubspot.com/marketing-
   statistics

Acknowledgements

Acknowledgements

With thanks to my mum and dad who taught me – by showing me – that success only comes if you work hard. To Lauren, for the constant stream of ideas and inspiration. Joe and Kerry, for being so generous with their praise and enthusiasm. Michelle Kane, my editor and friend, without your belief and support this book wouldn't have happened. I'm truly grateful to you for all of this; you've made one of my greatest dreams come true. To Naomi Mantin, my publicist: you have a wonderful energy and our vision feels perfectly aligned. Thank you to Iain Hunt for writing the politest emails and overseeing the final stages of the book. But also to everyone else at 4th Estate: the dream team. I'm honoured to be one of your authors. Danielle Pender, thank you for being so open in heart and mind (and for introducing me to Michelle).

And to Rich, my love, for cheering me on and never making me feel guilty if I need to focus on my career. You helped me to slowly find my feet as a freelance mum; I hope that this book will help others to skip ahead more quickly to success. Lastly, I'm grateful to my children, Joni and Bodhi, for presenting the challenges so that I could find the solutions and turn them into a book.